One hundred and ten percent

LEGEND

TONY KEADY

THE **OFFICIAL** BIOGRAPHY

One hundred and ten percent
LEGEND

TONY KEADY
THE **OFFICIAL** BIOGRAPHY

BY LIAM HAYES

HEROBOOKS

HEROBOOKS

PUBLISHED BY HERO BOOKS
1 WOODVILLE GREEN
LUCAN
CO. DUBLIN
IRELAND
www.herobooks.ie
Hero Books is an imprint of Umbrella Publishing

First Published 2018

A CIP record for this book is available from the British Library

ISBN 9781910827048

Printed in Ireland with Print Procedure Ltd
Cover design and typesetting: Jessica Maile
Cover photograph: Sportsfile
Inside photographs: Keady Family Collection, Sportsfile and Inpho

Contents

Dedication

For Tony Keady
Husband
Father
Hurler
Legend

Introduction

THE CALL FROM Tony Keady came out of the blue, and very far from the past, and when we met up two weeks later in The Clarion Hotel in West Dublin, just off the Galway road, I imagined shaking the hand of a man who had changed in 30 years. It was early February of 2017, a Saturday morning.

He was waiting for me in the hotel foyer.

In the car park, unknown to me, were Margaret and Shannon, and the three boys, Anthony, and Jake and Harry. The whole Keady clan. They were heading off to Liffey Valley Shopping Centre, as soon as Tony and I had finished talking. There was a Confirmation coming up, and a young man who needed to be decked out in the finest.

We talked and talked.

A good hour passed, and we entered a second hour, as Tony explained to me that he had decided to tell his story. He then began telling me that story, dwelling on the summer in New York that almost wrecked his career, and how it all ended, the Galway jersey almost being ripped off his back too soon after that summer. He wanted to publish his memoir. The whole shooting gallery of All-Irelands lost and All-Irelands won, and 'the affair.'

He wanted me to work with him on his book. He asked me would I write it? And he told me that he had something unbelievable to show me... it was in his car, and he'd show me when we were finished talking.

When I had walked into the hotel, that is just two miles from my home, I looked for a Tony Keady that would be, in all probability, older for starters, and wider. I expected to recognise about 50% of the man I had remembered from the old days, when he was a Galway hurler and I was a Meath footballer, and we had a habit of bumping into one another in 1987 and again in '88. Galway and Meath had won the All-Ireland hurling and football championships each of those years. We were a pair, and we found ourselves holidaying in The Canary Islands and in Florida. We actually found ourselves in the same hotels each January.

But Tony had not changed. He wore a tracksuit top over his jeans, and there wasn't a pick on him, not on his face, or anywhere else. He looked fit and strong, and ready to run out onto Croke Park.

Except I wasn't ready.

I told him that I could not work on his book, that I had a full publishing schedule for 2017, and I also warned him that 30 years was a long time. Would enough people want to turn around and journey back three decades to a time and a place where the Galway hurling team was top dog, and three All-Irelands in-a-row looked likely, before Tony Keady tore the backside out of that notion by playing illegally in New York and being banned for a year?

He was the most talked about hurler in Ireland all through 1989, even though he was banned from playing for even one minute in Galway's title defence. He was the reigning Hurler of the Year. He was still in his mid-20s, and it was expected that the second-half of his stunning career would be compulsive viewing also.

Except the remaining years of Tony Keady's career slipped and slided towards an ending that saw him considered used goods by his own county by the time he was 30 years old. The Tony Keady Story had everything, including a shooting star conclusion. I told Tony we would talk again.

And we did, several times on the phone through the remainder of the summer of 2017, his final summer.

We had all of the time in the world, as far as I was concerned.

Thirty years had passed, and what was another year or two? However, when our initial meeting ended, Tony had insisted on me walking with him to his car. I said hello to Margaret, Shannon and the boys, and then Tony opened the boot of his car. Inside were scrapbooks.

Except they were giant scrapbooks, like something Robbie Coltrane, the half-giant by the name of Rebeus Hagrid in the Harry Potter movies might have on the table in his hut on the edge of the Forbidden Forest. Tony explained that a friend had kept them, that he didn't want to cut out any articles with a scissors from any newspapers, and instead built the scrapbooks detailing Tony's career around whole newspapers. They were huge, and heavy.

Tony ordered his troops – Shannon, Anthony, and Jake and Harry – to start transferring them from the back of his car to the back of mine. They were too big to put on a shelf anywhere in my house. So I eventually took them from the floor of my office, and pushed them out of the way beneath a bed in a spare room.

That's where they remained and as the summer of 2017 sped by I forgot about them, until I read on that Tuesday morning, August 8, that Tony Keady was seriously ill in hospital after seemingly having a heart attack in his home the previous night. I decided I better throw my eye over the scrapbooks and be ready for Tony when he was released from the hospital.

For the next 24 hours I had no doubt that Tony would survive. No matter what had actually hit him, I told myself, he looked the strongest, the fittest and leanest 53 years-old man I had ever seen.

The next morning I read that Tony had died.

A few weeks passed and I telephoned Cyril Farrell, Tony's old manager from those glory days in the 1980s, and a long-standing friend of mine, and told him about the scrapbooks and asked him to return them to the Keady family. I wanted to get them back to the family fast. They are now too precious, I warned Cyril.

That same week Margaret phoned me.

And so, here we have Tony's Official Biography, a book that Margaret, and her daughter Shannon, and the three boys, wished to have published – because they saw this book as one of Tony's last great wishes in his life.

It has been a great honour for me to write *One Hundred and Ten Percent Legend*, and to spend time with Tony's family over many difficult and lonely months for them. I sincerely hope that building this book together has helped them that little bit in coming to terms with the absence of a husband and a father, who was as big in his own home as he was legendary in the eyes of GAA fans all over the country 30 years ago.

I'd like to thank all of Tony's friends and work colleagues for their support and encouragement and especially Patricia Treacy and Emer Hannon. I'd also like to thank Joe Canning, most especially, and also Conor Hayes, Gerry McInerney, Brendan Lynskey, Anthony Cunningham, and Tomas Mulcahy, for sharing their personal memories of Tony with me. And I'd like to thank Cyril Farrell for his role in guiding me and the Keady family.

The title of this book was, of course, very easy to decide upon.

Normally a book title is complicated, if not arduous. In my 23 years of publishing, the title of the book is usually the trickiest part – the 80,000 words inside are sometimes smooth going in comparison. But not this time.

I began to talk to Margaret and Shannon about the Will Smith post-apocalyptic movie, *I am Legend*. I told them that I thought we could play around with those words... perhaps even think of *I Was Legend*, and allowing the title to be in the first-person because, after all, Tony had a hand in the building of this book at the very beginning.

Margaret explained to me that Tony and Shannon first began to use the phrase '110%' with one another, but that he would also begin to ask any young or old hurlers he had with him in a dressing-room to never give less than '110%.'

He also asked this of his own family, and of himself.

'110%.'

As a legend Tony Keady was certainly nothing less than '110%'.

Welcome to *One Hundred and Ten Percent Legend*.

Liam Hayes,
April, 2018

THE MAN

THE MAN

MONDAY AUGUST 7, 2017, fought for all its might from earliest morning to be one of the happiest days in Tony Keady's life.

It was also his final day.

It was not a day for sleeping-in in the Keady family home in Oranmore, though everyone was still feeling the effects of the even longer, and truly exhilarating, maddeningly daft and fun-filled day that came before it.

Tony certainly had no intention of lying-in, either on August 7 or any other day. He liked to size up every single day and quickly set about extracting the fullest value from it. Margaret, of course, as always, was going to be out of bed before him. She liked to get her household jobs out of the way before the others rose. That way she would have all the time in the world to chat with Tony, and neither would she have to divide her time between chores and sitting down with the rest of them.

Shannon had a full, busy day ahead of her that included a camogie blitz at St Thomas' GAA club.

The boys, Anthony, and the twins Jake and Harry, typically had a dozen or more things, in a great big jumble, that they would want to get up and running. This included sorting through all of the old golf balls that they had claimed for themselves the week before.

Tony had brought his boys 'fishing' in the local golf club.

There must have been over one hundred balls in the bag, some of them dented and cracked, but lots of them brand new and as white and shiny as the day Titliest and Wilson had sent them off into the world to bring the joy of pars and birdies home for their smiling owners. Sorting through the bag of golf balls was high on the agenda for Tony and the boys, as was driving in to see Gerry McInerney, his old comrade-in-arms on the half-back line from the 1980s. Gerry's son, Gearoid had been named Man of the Match the previous day. Gerry needed to be congratulated. Tony needed to look Gerry in the eye and rejoice with him in glories past and, more importantly, glories being dug up afresh in the late summer of 2017.

'He had started golfing with the boys, and the four of them couldn't wait to get back out on the golf course,' Margaret remembers. 'They were sitting there on the floor in the front room, and the four of them were sorting through the bag.

'The craic they were having!

'Tony was in such form... I don't know how many cups of tea (Tony was not a coffee drinker) and coffee we had together that morning... and each time he wanted me to sit down and talk with him, but sure every time I sat on a chair, he was off... the telephone would go and he was gone, and I was saying to him each time, "Tony... you keep asking me to sit... and then you're away!" But it was the day that was in it.

'It was a day when every one of us was hyper.'

Margaret and Tony had decided to go for a walk. But Tony had to pick Shannon up from the blitz he had dropped her to earlier, so they decided to wait and talked about going to the cinema instead. It was just one of those days.

One that nobody wanted to see end, and one that needed to have so many delightful, memorable small events and memories packed into it. Galway were back in an All-Ireland final. Sunday, August 6, had seen to that.

Galway 0-22, Tipperary 1-18.

Tony wanted to do everything with his wife and children, but in the end Margaret and her husband realised that dinner needed to be put on the table. When the time came to prepare the dinner they would do so together, and Tony would hear no talk of Margaret dipping her arm into the freezer and retrieving a bag of frozen chips. Shannon would be starving after her long day, and he wanted his daughter and the boys to have proper potatoes. He started peeling the spuds and cutting them up. There would be no walk, no cinema.

Tony liked to take charge of his 'special dinners', especially on Saturdays when he would be the chef on duty. If it was steak and chips, then the chips would be very exactly built into towers for everyone and presented with aplomb. He'd have cut up onions and have rings also just right. If not steak, then Tony would let loose on his homemade curry. Saturday was Tony's day in charge – making sure the boys were showered before Mass, the twins' hair a perfect match.

But that Monday, Tony also wanted to go and see his brother who wasn't feeling all that well. There was a wedding coming up and Shannon had a county match hot on its heels, and Tony wanted to make sure that he would get to see his brother. Driving over to say hello to Bernard and chat with him about the game got priority.

They were with Bernard when they got a call to say that the dog was out. Tony and Margaret cut their visit short and came home to get Bingo, before they sat down to watch a movie. The whole family.

'He was laughing, and laughing,' Margaret continues. 'There was no sign... there was no ache, there was no pain... nothing.

'I'd have known with Tony if there was something wrong! He was in great form... wasn't he Shannon?'

Margaret looks at her 15 year-old daughter as she asks the question. Because Tony Keady and his only daughter were a pair. And it was Shannon, and Shannon more than Margaret, whom Tony would turn to if he was feeling any way off form.

'He'd always say it to me!' Shannon explains.

'If he was chesty or something, he would rarely tell the rest of them, but he'd say it to me.

'I'd say to him... "Dad, get something for it!"

'And then I'd tell Mam... but it was rarely he was ever sick.'

Margaret believes that if there was anything at all wrong with him that Tony would have spoken up.

'There was absolutely nothing wrong... nothing. We were conscious of getting up early the next morning because he was going into the school early. There was a camp in the school.

'Our routine on weekend nights was to sit down and watch telly for an hour, just the two of us when they were all in bed. We'd all go up the stairs together, but then, sometimes, himself and myself would come back down for that hour. If they were all in bed by half nine, then we'd come back down, but that Monday night we didn't come back down.

'Tony wanted to be up early.'

It was later than usual when the family went up the stairs. Half past ten, and all because of the day that was in it that so desperately needed to be filled with as much as possible. It was a day when all hands were on deck in the Keady household, almost every single hour, until half past ten.

Shannon and the boys had no school anyhow. What was the rush? There was a Pat Shortt movie on the telly. It was Tony who decided that the movie should be turned off. He also suggested to Margaret that they record the remainder of it, and watch it some other evening.

They were still on a high from the day before and the victory, but tiredness was settling in, boys were yawning, Tony was yawning, and even though none of them wanted the day after Galway's one point All-Ireland semi-final win over reigning champions Tipperary to come to an end, they all knew that Tuesday would be another day to feel so incredibly happy about life.

Sunday afternoon and the journey home that evening from Croke Park was not going to dim fast. Monday had lived up to everything asked of it. Tuesday was the next day that would have to deliver, but none of them had any doubts that any single day between the win over Tipperary and the All-Ireland final itself would fail them. How could one day dip into anonymity?

Not likely.

The journey home on Sunday evening had been slower than usual given the lines of traffic. When they got to the first toll on the motorway heading west there was a small degree of mayhem.

Mayhem that Tony saw as fuel for some wild celebration.

It began when some others in queuing cars spotted Tony Keady, the hero of the 80s, the former Hurler of the Year, the man who followed up that same year with a whole summer that was christened 'The Tony Keady Affair' and a summer that saw Tony banned from lining out with Galway in pursuit of three All-Ireland titles in-a-row. People started shouting at him.

Tony Keady, for once, was not in the mood for chatting. He wanted something wilder, and he started beeping the horn in his car. He soon lay his right hand on the horn.

'Tony started blowing,' Margaret recalls with a big smile, 'and then... everyone around us started blowing their horns. It was all a bit crazy, and I don't think anyone experienced it before trying to get through that toll.

'There was total noise... and people started putting flags out the windows and waving them. It went a little bit ballistic... and Tony had started the whole commotion.

'We were laughing and talking about it still the next day.

'And Tony was saying it was incredible, he'd never seen anything like it... and he was saying that we had to make sure we got six tickets in the same row for the All-Ireland final.

'He wanted us all together.

'I was saying to him... "Tony, don't bother about me"... because I was thinking about the cost of the tickets.

'But he said... "Don't worry, I won't go out for the next four weeks!" Even though all he ever had when he went out once a week was four or five pints anyway. But his big worry that Monday... his only concern in the world, was to get six tickets together for us all... so that we'd all be there.

'Together.'

•••◆•••

IN THE FIFTH minute of added time, out on the right touchline in Croke Park, Joe Canning had connected with the sliothar and measured from an impossible angle the winning point that would send Galway through to the All-Ireland final against either Cork or Waterford on September 3.

In a match that crackled the teams had been level 13 times through the afternoon. A replay seemed on the cards. Then Canning struck his eleventh point of the game, but there were still moments remaining and John O'Dwyer had one more opportunity for Tipperary but his effort from the right tailed off. The referee, Barry Kelly from Westmeath had seen enough. Galway had failed to score a goal for the third championship game on the trot but, what the hell... they were home.

It was the third year in succession that a semi-final between the two counties was decided by a single point.

Later, that same day, Tony Keady would tell his friends and old teammates, in addition to his family, that a one point win was the greatest victory of all over Tipp. One point had extra relish attached to it for the winners and, for the losers, and especially Tipp, it was a proper way to be executed.

One point was like one bullet.

It had been 1-10 to 0-12 at half-time, with Tipperary's goal coming from John McGrath, after a miscalculation by Galway goalkeeper Colm Callanan and his corner man Adrian Tuohy. The second 35 minutes did not deviate from the same script, pages turned speedily as point answered point.

Galway had been two in front, but Bubbles O'Dwyer and Noel McGrath pointed either side of a Canning '65' and 12 minutes from time John McGrath levelled. It was 1-16 to 0-19.

Canning pointed, but his score was cancelled out by McGrath.

There were misses too.

Galway finished with a total of 14 wides to Tipp's 11. But three minutes from the end Canning pointed after standing over a massive free from 90 metres out. Two minutes into added time Brendan Maher stepped forward. He tied the game with his strike from 70 metres.

Everyone settled on a draw match.

But there was another minute that forced everyone, including Tony Keady and his family, to sit tight. And another minute, and another, and then...

•••◆•••

TONY HAD A way of waking up his wife in the early morning, or even in the middle of the night, if he decided he wanted to have a word with her. He'd simply place his wristwatch next to her ear.

Without fail, Margaret would always awaken.

'TICK-TOCK'.

'TICK-TOCK... TICK-TOCK'

She hated that sound.

'Dad's watch had a really loud TICK-TOCK,' explains Shannon. 'He knew that was the way to waken Mam... just rest the watch beside her head on the pillow... and soon enough she'd be awake.'

For a few minutes Tony would imagine that there was something of great urgency, or else something that had spilled into his brain, that he needed to impart to his wife. He himself might have forgotten about it by morning.

So he'd rest his wristwatch near her ear.

And wait.

'There'd be something he might want to tell me... and then he'd turn over and go back to sleep himself,' explains Margaret.

That Monday night Margaret at first thought that Tony had placed his watch on her pillow, but that wasn't the case on this occasion.

She awoke, and told him that she was tired.

However, there was no watch next to her ear.

'Something woke me up!'

Margaret looked at her husband. Something was wrong. She thought at first he was having a seizure. He was distressed. Margaret had no idea what was happening, though in time it would be explained to her that Tony had succumbed to what is commonly known as Sudden Adult Death Syndrome. However because this affects infants and children too, it is formally known as Sudden Arrhythmic Death Syndrome, a term used to describe the likely cause of death in someone when a post-mortem examination has not shown any other potential cause of death, and when a structural heart disease or coronary disease or a 'hardening of the arteries' have not been seen or are not considered sufficient to cause death.

In the nearby bedroom Shannon woke up to her brother, Anthony who was standing next to her.

'SHANNON!' he shouted, '... THERE'S SOMETHING WRONG!'

Shannon and her brothers always brought their hurling sticks up to their bedrooms with them every single night. And at the bottom of each bed were the sticks that were the property of each Keady child.

Four children sleeping.

Four hurls at their feet.

'I was so tired that evening,' Shannon remembers. 'I had played in the blitz earlier in the day, and it took a while for me to awaken.' Shannon had her hurley at the end of her bed. She always brought it up to her bedroom, and always placed it at the bottom of her bed. She had the stick in her hand. She was confused, and did not know what was happening in the house.

'We are so fond of our hurls... we love them,' she further explains. 'And we don't want to leave them in the shed, and we never leave them downstairs either. We just don't want to leave them somewhere else.

'We always bring them up to bed with us.

'I don't know why I went into Mam and Dad's room... I should have run down the stairs after Mam... but I saw Dad and I thought he was asleep.

'Or I thought he got hurt... or something.

'But...'

Margaret was having difficulty talking to the emergency personnel on the phone. She was alarmed and shocked, and finally Shannon took over the conversation.

'They wanted us to put Tony on the floor,' explains Margaret, 'then we were doing CPR.'

Shannon took over that duty.

'Both Jake and myself had learned CPR at school.

'I tried it... and any time I went on the phone, Jake tried it.

'It felt like ages.'

It took 18 minutes Margaret Keady now says with certainty for the ambulance to arrive. Three vehicles arrived in total. Margaret tells Shannon that they could not have come to the house any faster.

••• ◆ •••

SHANNON KEADY HAD always enjoyed a special bond with her father.

She was Tony's only daughter.

Shannon says that she knows he loved his three sons just as much as her, but a special bond still developed between her and her Dad. She was the eldest in the family, and she was Tony's only girl.

Also, Tony and Shannon were 'similar.'

That's the word Margaret Keady uses to explain the relationship that developed between her husband and Shannon.

'The boys were in primary school,' explains Shannon, 'so I was always with Dad at secondary school. I would travel to the school with him in the mornings. And I'd come home with him... and then at lunchtime we were together.

'My locker wasn't always beside his room.'

Tony Keady worked as a caretaker at Calasanctius College in Oranmore, where he also coached the school teams.

'My first year locker was the furthest away from his little office. Second year I got closer and then... for third year I had a locker right outside his door.

'Usually I'd have lunch with Dad. I'd sit with Dad and Pat... and I also stayed for study in third year. Himself and Pat took turns waiting to lock up after school hours.'

When Shannon began taking supervised study after school Tony, when he came home, would tell Margaret that he could not eat his dinner.

'He was too lonesome coming home without her in the car,' Margaret adds, before Shannon explains just how serious her Dad was about feeding her and other students from the small fridge in his room.

'My favourite chocolate would be at the bottom of the fridge, and there'd be ham... if I didn't have food with me already before study.'

Tony also had biscuits. Lots and lots of packets of biscuits in case anyone was hungry. He didn't want anyone going hungry, most especially the hurlers manning the teams he was coaching.

'If you were hungry... and passing the room, you'd just go in and there'd be biscuits there on the table waiting for you,' Shannon recalls fondly.

•••◆•••

'TONY WAS FAR more than a school caretaker... that was probably the last thing on the list. He took on so many other roles during his time in Calasanctius. He did everything he possibly could for people. He was a coach, a mentor, a friend and an absolutely brilliant caretaker.

'You'd always hear him... ,' explains Patricia Treacy, an English and Religion teacher at Calasanctius College, and someone who, in her youth, cheered on Tony Keady.

'... before seeing him.

'You'd always see him walking down the corridors with something in his hand...he was always busy. He could turn his hand to anything. He was excellent at his job, incredibly talented, and he loved to show you what he had done and the great ideas he had... like when he kitted out the locker areas with shelving. He had painted them green and red, incorporating the school colours into his design... the colours that he was so proud to be a part of.

'He was always thinking outside of the box.

'Tony was such a positive person, vibrantly energetic and enthusiastic. He'd always be whistling, always happy. He had a special way about him, something that is difficult to describe in words. There was an innate goodness that emanated from him. His happiness was contagious. He instinctively knew if someone was upset or feeling down. He'd take time out of his hectic schedule to make sure that person was alright... be it a member of staff, a parent or a student. Tony would sprinkle his magic, use his witty words of wisdom, and put a smile back on your face.'

Patricia joined the teaching staff in the school a few years before Tony arrived at the turn of the millennium.

She remembers the school principal telling some of the staff that Tony Keady was getting the job as caretaker. 'She was very excited, but not as happy as I was. She knew she had someone important but I think she underestimated how important he was,' explains Patricia. 'I couldn't believe it. I could not believe that a childhood legend of mine was going to walk through the door.

'You would hear his phone, with its *Sunday Game* ringtone before you'd even see Tony. But once you heard the music you knew he was coming around the corner.

'He had nicknames for most of us... terms of endearment I suppose. Now, I'm glad he had them. They give us comfort today.

'I was 'Mrs Thrish... or 'Tisheen'... and we still carry on those names to this day, even though Tony is not with us anymore. It gave some of us great comfort when we came back to school in late August without Tony. We all knew what he called us each one of us, and we like to carry it on.

'And we were great friends... Tony and myself. My daughter, Saoirse and

Shannon are the same age, and I'd meet Tony at games... when Oranmore played our club Craughwell. Even though we were on opposing sides of the field, Tony would always come over and chat away with us, and have a laugh. He was such a gentleman and I was proud to know him so well

'He was a legend, everyone knew who he was, but I knew him personally. For that I am always thankful.

'Tony was incredibly selfless. He was so very considerate and kind.

'Last summer, we were playing against Oranmore in hurling. We were after winning, yet after the game Tony made his way across the field to speak to my son Aaron, who was the goalie. I saw him, walking across the pitch. I can still see his outline making his way over as Aaron gathered his hurls. He shook Aaron's hand and told him that he was a fantastic goalie and that he would man the goals for Galway one day, if he kept up the hard work.

'Aaron was beaming in the car on the way home.

'Sometimes people can forget the goalie, but Tony didn't. Tony forgot no one. He rang me after the game to tell me how good Aaron was and to wish us well in the rest of the competition. That was so Tony Keady. Even though his team had lost and his son was playing, he found time for us... for his friends, and to me that is truly amazing.'

A photo of Tony Keady remains on the altar in the school oratory.

There is also a book of memories. Stories that teachers and pupils have written down about the man who walked amongst them as a legend, a coach, a friend and their school caretaker.

There are so many stories, Patricia continues, that illustrate the kind-hearted and caring role that Tony sought to play in the lives of those he touched in the school.

'One young hurler, Seán has written in the book that he really wanted to impress Tony on the hurling field. Finally he got his chance as he was put into the forwards and the lad scored a great point.

'The second he did that, he looked over at the sideline to see Tony's reaction.

'He was so disappointed when he saw that Tony was on his phone... talking to someone. After the match when Tony told the young man it was a brilliant point Seán said he thought he hadn't seen it as he was on his phone.

That's when Tony told him that he was so thrilled with the point that he had rang the lad's mother there and then to tell her what her son had just done.

'And he had!

'When Seán met his mother, Ger a teacher in the school, she congratulated him. In the book of memories, the young lad has written that he will never forget that.

'That sums up Tony Keady. He was proud of everyone and made people proud of themselves.

'Tony was a big family man. Margaret and his children were the most important things in his life. He loved them deeply and often regaled us with their many victories both on and off the pitch.

'Himself and Margaret had a brilliant relationship.

'Working in the same building, they spent many hours together. They were like two teenagers, giggling and laughing. Margaret is our school secretary and his children, Shannon and Anthony are pupils in our school. He was looking forward to Anthony's team starting first year.

'He worked very closely with Pat Greally, our other caretaker. They were like two peas in a pod. They worked so well together and I know Pat misses him terribly. He also had a special relationship with our other two secretaries, Marie and Noreen. They were all solid friends, who spent a lot of time together whilst the rest of us were on holidays.

'They looked out for each other. Tony used to bring the *Advertiser* into Noreen every week. It's the small things, those thoughtful gestures that made Tony who he was and makes his loss all the more significant.

'He was a massive presence in the school, and when he passed away he left a huge wound... a gaping hole in everyone's lives in the school. As I said at the beginning, he was so much more than the school caretaker and a sports coach... he was the life and soul of our school.

'Our school motto is "Noblesse Oblige" meaning "To be the best that you can be." Tony lived that motto every day and, through praise and recognition, encouraged the students to live it too.

'Everyone loved him.

'He affected everyone... from students coming in for their first year, to the leaving Cert students. Even the children who did not know that he was a legendary hurler responded to his care and attention, and his wonderful personality.'

Tony knew that Gerry McInerney had been one of Patricia's favourite players on the Galway All-Ireland winning team of the 1980s.

'One day, he knocked on my classroom door and he told me that he had someone for me to meet. I stepped outside the classroom... and there was Gerry Mc. My childhood hero! I was lost for words. He had been into the school to see Tony about something, but Tony took the time to make sure that I got to meet him. I went home that evening, telling everyone that Gerry Mc came to see me.

'I still laugh at the memory. It was years ago.'

Tony's death had a profound effect on the entire school and student body. Emer (Hannon) was one of those students.

Emer is a champion boxer.

'When Tony saw her coming down the corridor towards him, he'd put his fists up and pretend to spar with her. He knew what all of the kids were in to.

'When Emer handed me her poem about Tony, it was unexpected. I was her English teacher but this wasn't an assignment. This had come from her heart and a need, in her, to capture the inspirational essence that is Tony.

'She wanted to express the huge figure Tony was for all of us, his importance in our lives and the deep, deep loss we feel now that the corridors are no longer filled with his laughter, his ringtone, his whistling.

'When I read this poem, I cried.

'To be honest, it still brings me to tears. I know, that in time, I will be able to read it without those accompanying tears. Tony affected us all. He will be forever missed and forever loved.

'Tony was a coach, a colleague and a really good friend.

'Tony was also an excellent caretaker; he certainly took great care of all of us.'

Keady

A community silenced,
Shock licenced.
The unique energy
Of the one and only, Keady.
Everyone listening
For a laugh now missing
That echoed the halls
And strengthened our walls.
A stellar example,
His humour was ample
He will be missed so
Ach tá a oidhreacht fós beo

Emer Hannon
August 10, 2017

•••◆•••

TONY KEADY WAS the youngest child in a family totalling 11 boys and girls brought into the world by their parents, Jimmy and Maureen. There was Noel, who also died too young, and there was PJ, Seamus, Petie, Brendan and Bernard. Six boys and then the girls, Phil, Annette, Teresa and Bridgie. Teresa would also die too young, and just four months after her youngest brother. Further loss would follow when Petie sadly passed away on March 10 in 2008.

When Jimmy Keady died on August 20, 1985, after a stubborn battle with emphysema that lasted almost two full decades, Tony was the only member of the family still living at home in Attymon. That brought with it responsibilities. But it also ensured Jimmy and Tony developed a loving and deeply caring relationship that stretched far outside the small circle normally occupied by an elderly father and his youngest son in rural Ireland.

Jimmy had lived just long enough to see Tony make his championship debut for Galway in that summer's All-Ireland semi-final, but agonisingly three weeks short of proudly viewing his son parade around Croke Park in the maroon No.6 shirt before Galway met Offaly in the final.

Tony could hardly remember a summer when his father was not unwell.

During those final handful of summers, if his father was feeling particularly weak, Tony would lift him out of his chair and carry him in his arms out the back door. He'd position his father in the front seat of his car, and they'd take off to whatever match was patiently awaiting the pair of them.

Carrying Jimmy Keady was sadly not at all taxing in the end, as the once strong man weighed five and a half stone.

'I'll park right behind the goals!' Tony would always tell his father, and he'd always rush in with the sucker-punch before Jimmy could... 'Safest place... nothing will hit you there!' For bigger games in Athenry or Loughrea, Galway county board secretary, Phelim Murphy would ensure that Tony's car had a direct route to the back of the nearest goals.

Cigarettes, slowly, and menacingly, brought down Jimmy Keady. He was on nebulisers every day. 'I used to always curse a calm day,' Tony recounted to the *Irish Independent's* Vincent Hogan in *Voices from Croke Park*, published in 2010. 'I reckoned he needed wind to give him a bit of breath.'

His father could barely walk. Any time Tony left the house without him, he made sure his mother had a phone number at hand in case he was needed back double quick. There was no good reason for Tony to fit into a fatherly role and tame Jimmy's smoking, even though he'd occasionally get a surprise when he pulled back the covers on Jimmy's bed and found Silk Cut boxes crushed and abandoned. Instead, when his father sat up in the same bed and asked for a light Tony would light a newspaper in the range and bring it up to him.

'Many's the time I nearly set him on fire!' Tony added in the same book.

Tony had just that one championship game under his belt when Jimmy Keady passed, but by then there had been plenty of thrills and spills on hurling fields all over the county, and Jimmy had seen his boy impress in plenty of foreign fields outside of Galway.

Jimmy had driven Tony to the field in which he claimed his first great prize as a hurler. What a prize!

It was only an under-14 tournament final in Salthill, in which Keady's

Killimordaly would have to battle with Mullagh, but the *Connacht Tribune* had very generously as sponsors decided against a set of medals or a large box of dodgy silver trophies that were equally common currency in GAA life. The newspaper decided to give a bike to every member on the winning team.

There were at least 20 of them, lined up on the sideline in Pearse Stadium, enough to make 13 and 14 year-old boys thirst like a man on a deserted island.

Killimordaly were awarded a '65' near the finish.

Bill Joe Creavin, one of the club's greatest and most trustworthy of mentors, thought to himself that young Tony Keady needed an extra incentive, and he made his way onto the field to sweeten a '65' that did not need any sweetening. Pipe in mouth he promised 10 shillings (a secondary prize that would never materialise) if Tony put the sliothar over the bar.

Tony Keady, like his own children, knew how to love a hurling stick. He would spend a goodly number of years after his retirement making sticks into magical instruments for boys and girls, women and men. A bandsaw and a planer, and a perfect piece of Irish ash – not your foreign stuff, God no... he wanted none of that cheap wood from the far side of Europe, Lithuania or God knows where – and Tony would spend hours at work before delivering a work of art fit for both pleasure and outright war.

As a 14 year-old with a bike on his mind, and the possibility of 10 shillings, though he had doubts about that from the moment he was challenged by Bill Joe, Tony also sought to have a stick in his hand that was that little bit superior to other sticks, and just right for him.

The handle of his hurl was cut straight across at the top, and on the top of it was a stone, taped on for extra grip.

The '65' won Tony and his teammates their bikes.

There was no fussy presentation. The boys pelted to the sideline to grab their new bikes and they cycled them from the ground to the Banba Hotel where there was a banquet of sandwiches and cocktail sausages. 'It was the biggest prize ever put up for kids at that time,' Tony explained.

'To us, it was like nearly getting a car!'

IT ALL BEGAN, in earnest, in O'Brien's Field.

And it began long before Keady and his mates were on their bikes. The national school bus had its stop at O'Brien's Field which was a deal prescribed by a hurling God. The person Up There even saw to it that there was a pump on the side of the road, just so that magnificent hurlers in the making could have easier access by vaulting over the same pump.

The school bags had already been tossed by the side of the road. Two sticks were always found pretty fast.

And someone would have been smart enough not to rely on divinity for simply everything. Baling twine would appear from a pocket and would be stretched across the top of the two sticks.

Tony and Tony's brother Bernard.

Eamonn Burke and Eanna Ryan and Gerard Hardy.

That was always one team sorted.

The ball was thrown in.

Tony Keady's career gathered pace at a rate of knots, with Killimordaly, the county under-16s, the Vocational School in Athenry, and by the time he won his first All-Ireland medal with Galway in 1983, on an under-21 team that defeated Tipperary, there was no doubt but that same career seemed to be in hurry. He had Pete Finnerty with him on that team, and also Ollie Kilkenny, Michael Coleman and Michael 'Hopper' McGrath.

And Eanna Ryan, still looking as sharp with a half chance as he did in O'Brien's Field and who came off the bench to help nail down that victory.

HOWEVER, WHEN GALWAY won the All-Ireland title for the first time since 1923, a 16 years-old Tony Keady was nowhere near the action. His father's emphysema had worsened. Tony sat at home watching the game, but he kept his fist tightened around the handle of his favourite hurl for the duration of the amazing game in which a Cyril Farrel-led Galway survived Eamonn Cregan's stunning tally of 2-7 and defeated Limerick 2-15 to 3-9.

It was 1980.

It was epic.

Bernie Forde collecting the ball two and a half minutes in and soloing through and kicking the ball past Tommy Quaid in the Limerick goal. Joe Connolly being fouled and pointing. Michael Connolly sending in a dangerous centre from the Hogan Stand side and PJ Molloy making no mistake. Galway leading 2-1 to 0-0. But there were no more goals for Galway. Eamonn Cregan's overhead strike connecting with a high lob for Limerick's first goal. A Cregan point, and another Cregan point, and a game for the ages was throbbing. Galway pointing and pointing and pointing. Cregan pointing. Galway pointing twice. Cregan and Joe Connolly trading points. John Connolly's bumper point from 50 yards out on the touchline. Galway reaching a five point advantage and it wasn't yet half-time.

It was a game Tony Keady would never forget. The game he wasn't at, and the homecoming that left him transfixed. 'It was hard to take it all in,' he remembered, 'the crowds... the Garda escort... the army, everyone out on the streets to see the team.'

Four years later, Cyril Farrell would see Tony Keady playing for the under-21s against the seniors in a challenge match. In his autobiography, *The Right To Win*, Farrell remembered noting 'good balance, was comfortable left or right and looked very, very confident.'

By the summer of 1985 Farrell was full sure that Tony Keady was ready. Seriously ready. Ready for the No.6 shirt on a championship team.

There was no turning back for manager or centre-back.

Even though only 8,200 people were bothered to turn up and take a look at Galway and Cork in the All-Ireland semi-final.

It wasn't meant to be a contest.

Who could blame them.

Cork were mighty Munster champs, defending All-Ireland champs, and it was raining cats and dogs.

Tony stood beside the taller, far mightier looking figure of Tim Crowley. He had just shaken hands with Crowley.

They were the hands of no man.

The property of King Kong, perhaps.

'I'm going to get eaten... and spat out here!'

Seconds in, and Crowley had pointed. Worse still, Tony had lost his footing as he took off in pursuit before the point.

A second ball came their way, and strangely the ball found its way beneath a particularly large divot. Both men started pulling.

The ball did not move.

Keady, eventually, connected. It was not the finest moment in his splendid career, nor the prettiest, but Tony Keady was on his way.

He was on his way and, once again, he was in a hurry. Three second-half goals from Brendan Lynskey, Joe Cooney and Noel Lane left Cork 10 points in arrears and listing badly. They did not go under, but there was no recovery. Tony was in his first senior All-Ireland final.

There would be four All-Irelands in quick succession. Two of them lost, Offaly first, Cork second. Two of them won, Kilkenny first, Tipperary second. Then there would be 'The Affair' in 1989. A fifth All-Ireland final that ended in defeat the following September. The end of Galway's greatest team of all time as Farrell stepped down.

And, finally, the weird, ridiculous, absolutely crazy termination of Tony Keady's career at 29 years of age.

HE WON HIS first Allstar award in 1986.

The following year he was beaten by a nose for the centre-back spot by Ger Henderson. In 1988 he was chosen as the greatest No.6 in the country a second time, and with that endorsement came something more.

Tony Keady was Hurler of the Year.

The best hurler in Ireland, bar none. The evening of the All-Ireland final he also won the Man of the Match award, but he was nowhere to be found when RTE's Ger Canning announced his name. Farrell had to step forward to accept the award on his behalf and suggest live on national television that Tony must already be training for 1989, which were prophetic words indeed.

Tony and his flatmate and 'hurling partner' Brendan Lynskey were back in their local public house, The Hut on Dublin's Phibsboro Road as RTE filmed the celebrations in The Burlington Hotel. The owner of the establishment had promised a champagne reception if Galway beat Tipp, and he was more than a man of his word, also dressing up his staff in maroon and white. Tony and Lynskey were firmly ensconced. A call from Farrell telling them to hop it to the hotel, and come in team shirt and tie, was ignored.

'Next thing the programme is on,' Tony recalled. 'Ger Canning with the microphone. It's time to name the Man of the Match. Everyone in the pub is going "SHHHHHH....".

'And Canning says, "It's the moment we've all been waiting for... the All-Ireland final Man of the Match is... TONY KEADY."

'Everyone in the pub goes ballistic, hugging each other. There's fellas hugging me who haven't a clue who I am. And the camera starts panning the hall in the Burlington, me about seven miles away.'

He was 25 years of age, but four years later on the afternoon of an All-Ireland semi-final he would be told that he did not merit a jersey minutes before the Galway team left their dressing-room.

Jarlath Cloonan had replaced Cyril Farrell as manager.

Tipperary, the biggest, boldest and greatest of enemies, were in the other dressing-room in Croke Park. But long before getting to that room, while the team spent time in the Phoenix Park pucking a few balls around in order to loosen up and ease the tension, Cloonan placed his hand on Keady's back.

'He said to me, "We're shortlisting you today." '

Tony had no idea what that meant.

He was dumbstruck, though the first thought that briefly elbowed its way into his head was that Cloonan was telling him he was going to captain the team against Tipp.

Then it dawned on him that it was not good news.

In the dressing-room he had on his boots, togs and socks, but no Galway jersey. As the team left the dressing-room Tony followed the rest of them out wearing only a jacket.

'Shortlisting you.

'That's how he put it.

'I'll never forgot the words.

'And that was enough for me.'

••• ◆ •••

MARGARET AND SHANNON and the boys made their way to Dublin the day before the All-Ireland final against Waterford.

As they always did with Tony.

And they stayed in the Regency Airport Hotel, which Tony always chose due to his long friendship with hotelier John Glynn. Before leaving Galway, however, they visited the grave.

Tony, at 53 years of age, had been laid to rest in Renville Cemetery in Oranmore, on the shores of Galway Bay. The previous day the Tipperary team and Babs Keating, their manager from those infamous battles in the 1980s were amongst those who queued for several hours to pay their respects to Margaret and the family. They were welcomed and hugged by Cyril Farrell and his now older, grey-haired team who had once convinced themselves that Tipperary were the ultimate enemy.

Farrell found the perfect sentence to sum up the indomitable figure of Tony Keady at No.6. 'He believed if there was 70,000 people in Croke Park then they came to see him playing.'

Of course the Tipperary men, and hurlers from all over the country, had very quickly realised soon after each of them decided to call it a day and end their careers, that the fiercesome figure of Tony Keady on the field was also a kind, gentle, extraordinarily friendly figure off the field. Clare's giant of a midfielder Ollie Baker was there. Brian Whelehan, the wiry and brilliant defender from Offaly, and Cork's strong-running centre-forward Tomas Mulcahy, who had spent so many of his days directly opposing Tony.

The Galway senior and minor teams, and their management teams, who had both qualified for their respective All-Ireland finals paid their respects. Tony Keady was a different generation but, through care and attention as a coach, and through his enormous love for the county teams, he had known all of them on those two teams. And all of them by first names, all of them the recipients of text messages from him before every game of importance.

Like everyone else in Galway and around the country, they had all waited for word after news broke that Tony Keady was seriously ill and was fighting for his life in University College Hospital. Twenty-four hours passed and when the tragic news confirmed that Tony had not made it, President Michael D Higgins spoke of his great sadness. 'He will be missed by all his colleagues in Killimordaly GAA club, and by the hurling and GAA community at large,'

Higgins stated. 'Sabina and I wish to express our deepest sympathy to his wife Margaret, his four children, and his friends and colleagues.' The safest estimate reached by the group of national newspaper reporters who attended the funeral was that 15,000 people filed past Tony's coffin.

After leaving their home for Dublin on the eve of the All-Ireland final Margaret first drove her family to Renville Cemetery so they could all have a word with Tony. Then they got back into their car.

Margaret and Shannon.

Anthony, and Jake and Harry.

And Tony.

'We had Dad's picture with us,' explains Shannon. 'We bring that everywhere we go now.'

The hardest part of the next 24 hours for Margaret was driving to Dublin. They always had so much to talk about when Tony was behind the wheel of the car. 'We went into Liffey Valley Shopping Centre, as we always did, when we got to the outskirts of Dublin,' continues Margaret.

'I had to sit down... I thought I was going to pass out.

'Everything was white...

'... through the loneliness.'

When they arrived at the hotel Shannon checked in on behalf of the family. They took the same room in the hotel that they always took before a big game in Croke Park. There, they sought to pull themselves together, to prepare for a Saturday evening they knew by heart but an evening that might now be something completely new and potentially overwhelming.

'It took us a couple of hours to be able to come back down the stairs. But... when we came down... it was not as bad as I feared. The same faces were there, Tony's friends... and the usual fun was there waiting for us.

'Brendan Lynskey was there... Pete Finnerty... they were all staying over as they always did, all of Tony's great friends. Our great friends.

'All of the friends he would have arranged to meet if he had been with us... they were all there, and we were so thankful to see every one of them.

'We had the same sing-song.

'They did it for us... and we did it for Tony.'

RTE KINDLY ORGANISED for Margaret and the family – who had also been guests on *Up For The Match* the previous evening – to be collected from their hotel the next morning. It was a large black mini van. With the family in the van was Pete Finnerty.

Margaret had asked Pete to be with them.

He was her first choice.

She had found out the day before the 2017 Leinster final, on July 1, when Tony gave a 'Legends Tour' in Croke Park to members of the public, that Pete Finnerty was also her husband's first choice.

Margaret and the children, and all of those who wanted to view the great stadium in the presence of Tony Keady, and revisit the great days and the disappointing days with him, were in one of the dressing-rooms. People were sitting and standing, and Tony was in the middle answering their questions.

'He was asked,' Margaret remembers, 'who was his No.1?... who was his favourite teammate? It was a difficult question, I thought.

'Because Tony had a great love for that team, and he had so many great friends on that team, but he was asked who was the man he would turn to if he needed to turn to one man?... and he had replied "Finnerty... Pete Finnerty!"

'I did not know that Tony would answer with Pete's name, even though when Pete had given the same Legends Tour in 2015 he had asked Tony to accompany him. Every one of them lads were so important to Tony, back then... and they still are, Eanna, Pat Malone, every one of them.

'I can still hear him say the name... "Finnerty... Pete Finnerty!" And that is why we asked Pete to come with us... and he was with us the whole day... he was the one we turned to... when we turned and instinctively wanted to ask a question of Tony.

'We could not have faced that journey into Croke Park on our own... have no one to talk to about the match.'

Margaret thought the whole afternoon went so agonisingly slowly, but Shannon thought the game a blur.

'It was difficult,' says Shannon. 'I could picture him sitting beside me, because for the semi-final... like we did for every match, we'd always argue to see who gets to sit beside Dad.

'At times that day... you'd think he was still there!

'At half-time I wanted to ask him how he thought things were going? Who's playing well... who's not?

'All of those little things.

'I was watching the two games and it kept going through my head, whenever a player got the ball... *What would Dad have said about that?*

'He might have said something like... *Ohhh... if he'd just jinked, if he'd done something else!*

'And all of the time, I was sitting there thinking... *What would Dad have said about that?... And what would Dad have said about that?*

'He might say... *That lad scored three points in his last match...* and we'd all watch that player more closely. He had a connection with all of them, and when every single player got the ball I was hearing Dad say something about him. He was always making comments.

'And Dad always had the Man of the Match picked before anyone else... and he was always right.

'We'd go to the shop and we'd come back with some stuff to eat... and...

'... it was just so hard to find that he wasn't sitting there with us.'

Margaret had an uneasy feeling in her stomach when she arrived at the ground, and it persisted through the minor final. She feared the minor team would lose to Cork, and it did look like a Cork victory was totally on the cards at one stage.

'We were sitting down with Pete, inside, in one of the lounges,' says Margaret, 'and Anthony came in and he said, "The minors are being hammered!" And I thought... *We'll go out, and watch them!*

'And as soon as we were sitting outside the game turned around, and when I saw Sam McArdle and Shane Ryan come on... that was the icing on the cake, because they were on the school team with Tony. I knew Tony wanted them to win... and they did!'

The Galway minors conceded two early goals. They were six points down to a Cork team that were well fancied to begin with that morning.

But two goals from Jack Canning, a nephew of Joe Canning, in the 32nd and 39th minutes gave Galway a one point lead, and more than a sniff of a memorable win. They would do so, in a thriller, 2-17 to 2-15.

'They came back and I thought... *My God, Tony...* and I was looking at

TONY KEADY: THE OFFICIAL BIOGRAPHY • THE MAN

Shane and Sam... and I kept thinking... *Tony!*

'Tony would never have missed any of the minor matches. He knew all of those young lads... from our own school...and when we played other schools. He loved all of those young lads.

'He knew every one of them inside out. Even at the beginning of the season and they were leaving Oranmore for Cork... for a game... it was a game we didn't go to.

'Shannon had a match and we couldn't drive down to it, but as the Galway bus was driving away Tony was there at the roundabout.

'He was there with his big hand in the air...

'Waving them off.'

MARGARET BELIEVES THAT her husband had the phone numbers of every single Galway hurler on his phone, boy and man.

'Padraic Mannion, Cathal Mannion, Jason Flynn... you could go down through the team list, and he'd be in touch with them all the night before the game.

'Good luck tomorrow' he'd text them.

'But it wasn't just a group text,' insists Margaret. 'He would send an individual text to each lad with a special message on it.'

••• ◆ •••

THE SENIOR FINAL left just three points between Galway and Waterford, but unlike the game before it the men in maroon were concentrated and powerful, and seemingly unnerved, from the moment the ball was thrown in.

They won 0-26 to 2-17.

The final scoreline did not tell the true story of an absorbing game. Waterford claimed their two goals in the first-half, but when they dearly needed at least one more they found the shutters pulled down in front of Colm Callanan's goal.

In added time there was a late scramble on the edge of the square, and a mild panic rose in the throats of the Galway supporters. Simply put, Galway had too many bigger heroes throughout the afternoon.

David Burke fired over two points in each half from the middle of the field. Gearoid McInerney had the measure of reigning Hurler of the Year Austin Gleeson.

And Joe Canning shot another nine points.

That was 20 in total over the final two games of the season from perhaps the most humble, but definitely the most outstanding hurler in the country.

Galway had waited 29 years for ultimate hurling glory. Waterford had to crane their necks further back to 1959 for the last occasion when the Liam MacCarthy Cup was carried home. Both counties were thoroughly deserving, and Tony Keady would have loved the mischief, and the tactical genius, of both managers, Micheal Donoghue and Derek McGrath.

McGrath had Tadgh de Burca, who had missed the semi-final win over Cork, drop from wing back into a role sweeping his own defence, and McGrath also had Darragh Fives, who wore No.15, also fall back deep.

McGrath went with five up front.

Donoghue had Aidan Harte as his team's extra man in defence.

Tony Keady, no question, would have had lots to say about what he saw presenting itself in front of him.

But Harte was largely untroubled in the beginning as he watched the men in front of him shoot nine points, some of them sublime, others brazen if not breathtaking, before Galway disappointed with their first wide. Kevin Moran's fourth minute goal kept Waterford from dropping their heads. Suddenly, in the 22nd minute, the teams were level with Kieran Bennett – McGrath putting him in at wing-back just before the game in place of the selected Darragh Lyons – finding the net with a long ball from the Cusack Park touchline that befuddled both defenders and forwards in front of Callanan.

The 2017 All-Ireland final was alive.

Galway after all their work standing at 0-10.

Waterford waking up to 2-4.

But McGrath lost Shane Bennett to injury.

Maurice Shanahan thundered in spelling trouble, but in the process McGrath had lost his chief impact substitution.

Once such blistering starts are unceremoniously brought to heel, teams in All-Ireland finals often freeze. But there was not one chill in one Galway bone. They had seven players on the score sheet before half-time. Confidence was in flow. That, and Joe Canning, who fired over a free just before the half-time whistle to once more give Galway top billing on the scoreboard, 0-14 to 2-7, meant that Derek McGrath would have to start all over again in the tiny interval window to out-think Micheal Donoghue.

Donoghue had spoken to his players about Tony Keady in the quiet of their dressing-room before the game.

So too did Derek McGrath in the rival room.

Galway were open to Tony's help.

Waterford respectfully wished him to mind his own business.

When it was all over, Margaret Keady stood in the middle of the field with Shannon. Joe Canning, the hero of the day and also the whole glorious year when Galway claimed absolutely every single trophy available, stood between them as the rest of the Galway players celebrated up the steps of the Hogan Stand.

'I can't remember enough about that day at all,' confesses Margaret. 'But I can remember Joe standing with us and... he had tears in his eyes.

'I still feel that Galway won with Tony's help. They are a great team, and they played brilliantly.

'But Tony had extra powers working for him, up there... Above.

'And when I watched the minor match, I said to myself...

'Oh my God, Tony is here!'

•••◆•••

THEY HAD MET for the first time 29 years earlier, at that time when Galway were last All-Ireland champions.

1988.

Margaret and Tony met in Meath, the home of that year's All-Ireland football champions. Margaret Curran, therefore, was a football fan and not a hurling fan, but when some of the Galway hurlers were asked to come and dine with some of the Meath footballers in Rathcairn, Margaret's homeplace, and Meath's Gaeltacht, she was working behind the bar in the local community centre.

The actor Mick Lally, a man with a love for the native tongue, was also invited that same night, and the star of the stage and also RTE's soap *Glenroe* sought to help Margaret when she cut one of her fingers on a broken glass. 'He had a few pints on him,' Margaret recalls, 'and he was plastering every finger except the right one, it seemed.'

Tony Keady stepped in, and suggested that he would be able to do a better job than Lally. Margaret and Tony spoke for the first time.

But everyone, and particularly a lot of other Meath lassies were flocking around Tony. Margaret had no time for that carry-on.

But whenever she looked behind her and into the kitchen at the rear of the bar, it seemed that Tony was there, looking to avoid most of the attention elsewhere. Despite remaining extra proud, Margaret thought nothing wrong with dreaming up excuses to walk by him any time she went to fetch more glasses. There wasn't very much said that night, because three years slipped by.

'I was with a chap... and we walked into The Shawl.

'I didn't know that much about Galway. I had started working in Spiddal, and I didn't know Tony and Brendan Lynskey were running their own pub. I walked in and saw the two of them, and I thought Tony was the barman.'

They chatted.

The next night, Margaret asked to be brought back to The Shawl. 'I made sure I went back... and I stayed with Tony the rest of the evening.'

Margaret was still a football woman. She hadn't paid any attention to Galway's woes, and Tony's ridiculously harsh 12-month suspension in 1989 for playing under a false name in a championship game in New York.

That all went over head.

All the back page news day after day, and when the story made the front pages of newspapers also it travelled at 30,000 feet above her. Margaret still remained none the wiser of the whole Shakespearean-like tragedy that was befalling her future loving husband.

They started going out together in September of 1991, and they were married on January 5, 1996. In the early years of their courtship there was still a good deal of attention paid to Tony, and attention often equalled commotion, and Margaret still considered that a carry-on that she could do without.

'There was still a fuss being made of him,' she fondly says, 'but he told me not to let any of it get to me.

'I used to tell him... "I don't want to be part of this, Tony"... I couldn't stand the crowds really, and all that fuss. But, whatever the occasion... or wherever we were, Tony always made me feel important.

'We were on our way to Meath, when he proposed to me. We were on the bridge in Birr, but whether I was important to him... or not, there was no such thing as him getting down on one knee or anything like that.

'He was driving over the bridge when he proposed to me.

'We were coming from Portumna, and he handed me the ring... and he said, "Put this on your finger!"

'Granted he had slowed down the car when he handed me the little box.

'He had it in his mind to get engaged the week before the Galway races, but my mother had died. He decided to put it off till nearly Christmas. He was waiting to pick his moment... and he had the box in one of his pockets since July.

'Whatever spurred him, he decided at that moment... on the bridge in Birr, and he kept talking, telling me... "I'm not going to be hanging around, forever engaged... and we don't want a big wedding.'

TONY DIDN'T WANT any invitations sent out.

Neither did he feel it necessary to ask his brother, Noel to come home from America because, in Tony's eyes, that was a whole lot of unnecessary expense and for what? Margaret replied 'Fine' when Tony knocked the invitations on the head.

'Anyone who wants to come... can come!' he stated.

Margaret agreed.

As for his Best Man?

'The first fella to walk through the door of the church in a suit... he's getting the job!' Tony stated.

Margaret did not argue.

'If my mother had been alive, then it would have been a completely different day,' Margaret now explains. 'I had no sisters, just my two brothers and two lovely sisters-in-law who were both pregnant. I went off on my own shopping for my dress.'

Though that was not strictly true.

'Myself and my three years-old niece, Katie went into McElhinney's in Athboy to buy my dress.

'She sat on a little box in the store.

'She was so small, but she was an honest little girl... and she remained sitting on that box as I put on dress after dress. And each time I came back out and looked at her, she'd shake her head.

'Then I put on this dress that also had a little jacket and, thankfully, Katie did not shake her head. She looked back at me and, then... she moved her head up and down. That was the dress I bought. She was a very special little girl, and she is still a special woman in my life.'

The sum total of 28 people attended the wedding of Margaret and Tony. The invitations never manifested themselves, and one of Tony's sisters stopped in a shop on the way to the wedding to get her outfit. The job of Best Man was awarded to Sean Nevin who worked with Tony in his hurling making business. Tony had had a quiet word with him after all.

But that was it.

There was no other big drama, and when one of Margaret's brothers, Gerry got backed up dosing cattle on the morning of the ceremony Tony jumped in to give him a hand. Gerry was supposed to be driving his sister to the church, and Gerry had a reputation in the Curran household for being late for practically everything.

Tony didn't want the pair of them to be late.

'Tony really went out and helped him in order to hurry him along. The next thing the vet arrived, and he took a look at the stranger, and asked... "Are you Tony Keady? What are you doing up these parts?" '

Tony told him he was getting married.

The vet enquired... 'When?'

'Today!' Tony told him.

'About an hour's time!'

Tony had not purchased a suit for the occasion himself.

He wore his favourite sports jacket and slacks.

'He was so laid back, but it looked lovely on him. He was like my father in that way, Tony and my father were a pair and when my father suggested to us that he would give us the money for a new car, rather than spend the same money on a great big wedding... well, it could have been Tony talking.

'My father said he didn't think we should spend money on a day that's gone up in smoke so fast, when we could have a brand new car.'

Sean Curran and Tony Keady were in absolute agreement.

Margaret too. 'It was a great investment and thank God, we were able to have a new car always after that start. But we had a great honeymoon. We went off for three weeks... to Florida, and we had an amazing time. It was my first sun holiday. Tony had been out there with the Galway hurlers.

'We had our home built by then too, even if we had nothing in it.'

Margaret and Tony were set for life.

For a long life together.

•••◆•••

MARGARET WAS IN a lounge in the Hogan Stand when she was approached by one of the officials on duty and asked if she would like to go out onto the pitch after the game? If Galway won, and David Burke was receiving the Liam MacCarthy Cup would they like to view the presentation from that precious vantage point?

Margaret knew it would mean everything to her three boys and Shannon.

She thought back to the 'Legends Tour' in the middle of the summer. On that afternoon, Anthony and Jake and Harry were dying to run out onto the field, that was out of bounds to visitors.

After the final whistle to the 2017 All-Ireland final, Margaret and Shannon and the boys were escorted down from their seats, and in a flash the Keady boys ran off with Michael Donoghue's children across the sacred grass.

There were heroes in sweaty maroon jerseys to be seen from up close, and they were not hard to find. Actually, Gearoid McInerney and some of the other 'heroes' took personal care of Anthony and Jake and Harry.

Colm Callanan looked after Harry.

'He is going to be a goalkeeper,' promises Margaret, 'And he has everyone

45

giving him lessons. John Commins is teaching him, and Davy Fitzgerald has promised him some lessons. He is fearless... and he is good.'

Shannon arrived down onto the pitch and found herself alone and upset for a moment. She was looking around at everything, engulfed by the noise and the drama, and then Joe Canning gave her a hug.

They started talking.

The presentation of the cup was underway in the stand in front of them, and Shannon was looking up and time passed, and she suddenly realised that Joe Canning was still standing by her side.

Canning and Micheal Donoghue were in no rush to leave Margaret and her daughter. The Galway supporters on Hill 16 began to chant. Shannon began to tell Joe how well he had played and was congratulating him. He told her that he was still in shock, and that he could hardly believe Galway were All-Ireland champions, but then he changed the subject.

Joe told Shannon to turn around, and listen.

He told her they were calling out her father's name.

'KEADY...

'KEADY... KEADY.'

Joe Canning, Galway's greatest hurler on the greatest day of his career, gave Shannon another hug as they listened to Tony's name echoing across the pitch and towards them both from the Hill.

In the sixth minute of the game the Galway supporters had been joined by everyone packed into the stadium in a round of applause; the sixth minute appropriately reminding everyone of the man who once wore the No.6 maroon shirt. And at half-time the GAA paid a further special tribute with a three and a half minute video of Tony's career that included tributes from Pat Malone, Pete Finnerty, Pearse Piggott and Eanna Ryan.

But the Galway supporters wanted to remember Tony some more during their celebrations.

Joe told Shannon... 'That's all for Tony... everyone loved him!'

'He was not going up for the presentation,' Shannon now recalls, revisiting the exact moment and experiencing the same amount of panic that visited her at the time.

'They were lifting up the cup.

'I told him... "Go up Joe... You need to go up."'

'I kept telling him he should be up there...

'... with the rest of the team... "Joe... Go up!"'

'He kept saying "No"... that it was okay, that he wanted to stay where he was...

'... with us.'

•••◆•••

THE CANNING FAMILY had lived close to Tony's workshop in Gortanumera, outside Portumna.

Tony was a maker of quality hurleys.

And a young Joe Canning, at a time when he struggled to stretch to Tony's chest – even when he stood on his tippy-toes – was a boy who wanted the very best stick Tony could make. In time, Tony would leave the business, and shortly after he did so the Canning family would become one of the most notable suppliers of sticks to teams in Ireland, and to hurlers all over the world.

Tony was still working in Gortanumera when he married Margaret, but when Shannon was on the way Tony told his wife that he felt the hurling season was too limited. Also, he was finding it more difficult to get his hands on good Irish ash. 'He was not going to make someone a hurl from wood that came from Lithuania, as he said himself, or wherever... if it was not Irish ash it was no good for Tony,' explains Margaret.

They decided to leave the hurley making business behind them, and enter the 'family business' with even greater commitment.

March to September, when the demand for sticks was highest was fine, but what about the rest of the year?

That was Tony's question.

He wanted a steady job, guaranteed income. Tony and Margaret knew that everything was about to change for them. It was 2001, and Tony said he might continue to make a few hurls now and again, but he called a halt to his eight year-old business, and took up his job as a caretaker in Calasanctius College in Oranmore, where Margaret would also work. Tony also changed

47

because of impending fatherhood. When Tony and Margaret's first born was a daughter, Tony changed even more. He embraced his new role with gusto, and the attachment between Tony and Shannon from day one was clearly made of the deepest love and admiration.

Before then, however, and while Tony was working full-time at measuring and balancing perfect hurleys, Tony and young Joe Canning got to know one another very well indeed.

'Joe would always go down to his workshop,' Margaret explains. 'and Tony would come home for the dinner...and he'd say... "That Joe Canning... I got nothing done today, because he was down with me the whole time." '

Margaret knew her husband was not complaining.

The young boy had something about him.

Already, there was a magical quality about how he talked about the hurley he wanted, and how fussy he was about having it just perfect.

'Dad would tell the story,' Shannon continues, 'about how he would drive past the school that Joe was in... and Joe would be looking out for him.

'Joe would be peering out from behind the big gates.

'And Dad would find himself beeping the horn... and Joe would get a lift home with him, because the families lived so close to one another. Every time he turned the corner in his car, he told us he would always see that... "Blondie head of Joe Canning."

'Dad always said Joe was so fussy.'

Margaret nods her head.

And she smiles. 'Joe was so particular about his hurls, even as a little kid... and I suppose he looked up to Tony as well as a famous hurler... as a Hurler of the Year... something Joe would also become.

'Tony made so many hurls for Joe, and Joe... he was always so fussy.

'So fussy.

'He might spend the whole day in the workshop with Tony... and he'd be picking the plank, and watching everything Tony was doing. And y'see, Tony would always give time to anyone, but especially children. I don't believe Tony even needed a watch because he would never check it, and yet... he'd never be late for anything.

'He always made sure he had time for people... for kids.

'Time for everyone, and everything... but he'd gladly give his whole day to young Joe and he'd come home, into the kitchen to me, and there'd be a big smile on his face and he'd say... "That Joe Canning!"

'Joe always picked out his own plank of wood.

'It had to be just right, and Tony would know that the boy would pick the perfect plank.'

JOE CANNING LAUGHS at the same memory.

'Tony worked with Sean Nevin, his brother-in-law, and their place was only 200 or 300 yards from our school,' Joe recalls.

'They made the hurleys together. Like back then, I always used their hurley... he was the only hurley maker as well as anything else around these parts.

'I'd go into them, and I'd be fussy alright... I have to admit to that.'

Joe has another memory of Tony that he says is 'huge.'

He was in the national school in Gortanumera, a tiny school, so tiny that there were only five other boys in his class, but they made it through to a school final. They were playing Ballyturn.

And they would win the game easily, 6-7 to 1-1.

But the memory is not of the victory and the happiness afterwards. Instead, Joe still recalls being amazed that one of the most famous hurlers in the country turned up to watch and, not only that, but that Tony Keady was more than willing to serve as one of the umpires.

'Tony had a nephew on the team... Colin Nevin was playing with us, Sean's son... and Tony was umpire that afternoon. For someone like him, who was a complete hero to us... for him to turn up and do umpire was pretty cool. And we were only a small school, it was a two-teacher school... and we only had numbers for seven-a-side hurling.'

Joe revisits his time in the workshop. 'Yeah... I would go up to his workshop, and I'd watch what they were doing... and I'd be fussy enough.

'I still am, I suppose.

'But Tony and Sean would make the hurley for me.

'It was probably not all day I was with them. My mother would want me home anyhow, but I would have been with them for long enough... longer than every other kid like me or some other Joe Soap who came in for a hurley.

'I remember they would have a few nice ones left out for me... I suppose that way I'd only be getting in their way half the time.'

Joe was not one of the Galway players whom Tony would text before games. It was not necessary when Joe Canning reached the high point of his career as a Galway hurler and was chasing what seemed a damned elusive All-Ireland senior title. They would meet regularly. Joe was living in Oranmore, like his old hero, and they'd bump into one another in the shop or the petrol station all of the time.

'Tony didn't need to text me before games and wish me luck,' Joe asserts. 'He would have shaken my hand and told me to my face.'

Typically, Joe makes absolutely no big deal of spending possibly the most precious few minutes of his career with Tony's wife and daughter once the 2017 All-Ireland final had delivered everything it promised.

He explains that it happened... 'naturally enough.'

'Margaret and Shannon came onto the field... and they walked in behind Micheal Donoghue and myself. I had already met my own family in the stand, and when we saw Margaret and Shannon it was just a natural thing to do...

'And so we stood beside them.'

The gesture transcended an epic All-Ireland final, and left a watching nation absolutely transfixed – at the kind-hearted gesture that silently articulated the true nature of the GAA at a time when the association is being accused of becoming some form of crazed commercial beast. But Joe Canning says there was no talk between anyone on the Galway panel or management team to embrace the Keady family on such an historic and emotional day.

'There was no plan, and it was no big deal for us to do what we did,' Joe further explains. 'Shannon is friends with my niece, Tegan... they were on the Galway team together... played in the under-16 All-Ireland camogie final.

'It was not as if it was something Micheal and myself thought we should do. It was just the natural thing.

'I didn't realise any significance to it.

'It just happened, and it was good if it helped them.

'Anyhow, we had been close to the family all that time. We had Shannon and the three boys, Anthony and Jake and Harry, in with us at training the week before the final... just in... pucking around with the lads and taking some shots. The evening they were in with us I wasn't training myself because of my knee... I needed to rest it before the game... so I didn't puck around with them myself.

'We knew it meant something to Margaret and Shannon to be with them after we won, and we wanted them to realise that Tony was with us in our thoughts that whole day. He was a huge part of Galway hurling history and his performances in All-Ireland finals inspired so many people.

'I hoped it helped them, the same as thinking of Tony definitely helped us as a group of players.'

Joe also reveals, with typical honesty, that he had no intention of walking up the steps of the Hogan Stand, and joining with his teammates in a tribal celebration as the Liam MacCarthy Cup was finally handed over to them, and trusted in their possession once again after 29 long years.

He has always been one who prefers to stay on the field at times like that, and the aftermath of the 2017 All-Ireland final was no different.

'I don't know why I did not go up onto the Hogan Stand.

'I don't know if I ever went up those steps... maybe after our first All-Ireland club title, but ... to be honest, I like to get to see my family straight after the game and stuff like that.

'That is more important to me.

'Some people like to do it, and walk up those steps... and it's not that I don't want to do it, or wouldn't like it.'

He remembers Shannon Keady telling him that he should leave her, and go join his teammates.

'But my priority after a game has always been to stay with the people I know... my family and my friends.

'I can see how it is nice to be up there celebrating and receiving a trophy... but at a time like that everything can be a bit of a daze... and I like to hold onto the memories.

'It's nice to have a clear memory of watching it all happening in front of you. And get that chance to take it all in.

'At least try to take it all in!'

•••◆•••

TONY WAS A rebel *with or without causes.*

Such was the popular theory during his days as one of the greatest Galway hurlers of all time, though it was without any credible foundation.

Of course, he liked to huff and puff as some sort of James Dean-type character in the famous movie of the '50s, *Giant*. But Tony had a deep respect for people, and he always valued knowledge, and learning.

His wife says he loved school as a boy.

And as a grown man, and a former hurler who had found fame in every county in Ireland, he never failed to greet one of his former teachers with the title 'Mr X' or 'Mrs Y'. In particular he loved maths.

'One thing Tony never lost was respect for others,' insists Margaret.

His daughter remembers how he would always tell her and her brothers how he was taught a particular subject. Usually maths.

'He'd be doing maths homework with us at the table, right here,' Shannon adds, 'and he'd say... "Gerry Aherne taught it to me like this!"

'But then they changed the maths curriculum,' says Shannon.

Tony hit a brick wall.

But he instantly decided to find a way around the same wall.

Whenever he came across one of the maths teachers in the school and he thought them free for a little while perhaps, he'd request some personal tuition.

'Tony would ask,' explains Margaret, 'and he'd say... "Can I have ten minutes?"

'Tony wanted to get ahead of our own children.'

It worked.

Whenever Shannon found herself stuck in her homework her father would be on hand with his own copybook.

Tony Keady!

Yes, Tony Keady would produce his own copybook!

'He'd get his own copybook out,' says Shannon, 'and make sure I got through it, and make sure I was a step ahead of the class the next day.'

Rebel indeed.

THE LEGEND

LEGEND

CHAPTER 1

1985

CONOR HAYES AND Tony Keady would take time out together to practice their free-taking. Each man stood on a 21 yard line, and demanded the very best from one another. Except Hayes liked to make it extra personal.

He'd dare Tony to land the ball on his hurl. Not just reach him with the ball or get it close enough to the other man down the other end of the field.

On the hurl.

'We'd both be out there... on the respective 21 yard lines, belting the ball.

'He'd hit it and it might be almost a beauty... and I'd be telling him that he was miles off. But usually, in truth, he'd be hitting me most of the time.

'I'd keep kidding him, and make him want to hit me... and then before games I'd be telling him not to be nervous taking the frees... telling him that I'd take them if he didn't feel he was up to it.

'He'd never want me to take any of them of course.'

Hayes first shared the field with Tony in 1984, when the seniors played the under-21s in one of their usual training games. It was a useful test for both teams, and especially the under-21s who were left in a bit of a vacuum, waiting and waiting, and watching the Leinster and Munster championships work their way to a conclusion. Games were hard to come by for the under-21s.

Always was, even back in Conor Hayes' underage years.

That afternoon in '84 Tony played centre-forward. Afterwards, Hayes remembers having a few words with him, but one of the heroes from Galway's historic 1980 All-Ireland triumph had no real idea what would become of young Tony Keady. When Cyril Farrell brought Tony into the senior squad the following spring, Hayes had a good second look.

'Farrell brought him in to us in '85 and launched him quickly. He took to it, and I said to myself... *this fella has something.*'

Most of the senior lads in the dressing-room had something to say about Tony when he got to work on the old warrior Tim Crowley in the 1985 All-Ireland semi-final, and barely flinched in putting in a performance that any veteran would have been immensely proud of. PJ Molloy was the first to have a quick word in Hayes' ear after that brilliant victory.

'I remember PJ Molloy saying to me... "This fella better be careful... he'll be in danger of going from hero to zero!" Because he was that good against Tim Crowley, and if you can be that good against Crowley then that created a huge expectation... and what if the next man he played against got a good few scores against him?

'What if he went out against Offaly in the final, and had a bad day? That was the only danger, we thought. We chatted about it at the time, but it never happened. You see, no one had heard much about him before that... and suddenly he was elevated to 'greatness' after just one game.

'PJ just said to me... "This fella needs to be careful... a bad game and they might fleece him in the papers."

'But, as I said... we needn't have worried for him!'

Hayes, from the vantage point of the full-back position, had a prized view of Tony Keady's arrival onto the Galway senior team, and the excellent performances that totted themselves up thereafter.

He says that Tony was a 'joy' to watch all of those years.

'He was an outstanding man to play behind. He had it all, but his positioning was incredible... knowing how to play the game and where to be came so naturally to him. He'd be there in the right place, and he'd clear the ball under pressure... maybe 70 or 80 yards down the field.

'There was no 20 yard taps to a teammate in our day when you were getting the ball out of defence.

'In league games he might tune out a little, but he'd be laughing at us afterwards when any of us asked him what happened? He'd more or less say... "What is there to be worrying about in a league game!"

'But, we would keep onto him... myself and Finnerty... we'd bawl him out of it on the field at times. It happened in games he thought were not all that important, or in early league games... in any of those games if he was going very well then you might see him tune out that bit.'

Tony liked to give his teammates the general idea that he was a free spirit, unaffected by the pressure that they all felt building up all around them as the year ploughed on towards August and September.

'He liked the bravado.

'But he cared alright. You just had to look at the way he presented himself, he was in amazing condition.

'We'd turn the blind eye now and then when he did not turn up at training. Cyril Farrell was good at managing him in that way... he'd know when to come down on him hard... and when to leave him alone.

'He'd like us to think that he was in the pub... he dared us to come to that sort of conclusion, just so that he could prove us wrong the next day. He told us on one occasion that he got injured falling off a trailer of turf, for instance... when we all more or less knew that he was playing a game of soccer.

'He was a natural and he never had to try too hard. It all came naturally to him. That was part of who he was... that enigmatic thing about letting on he was out on the town and acting the mick... when really he was minding himself all of the time.

'But Farrell was happy for Tony to be his own man at times like that, and the rest of us... we'd wait till the game was over before deciding the truth and what should be said to him.

'He never let us down when it mattered.

'Most of the time I felt a relief to have him in front of me. When he got the ball, no matter what pressure he was under... you knew that it would land down the other end of the field.

'He played a very open game alright, but I got use to that quickly. He always liked to play an expansive game. He prided himself on that and wanting to be the best he could possibly be, and we never had any doubt about him when we went out onto the field.'

Hayes could see that Tony knew no nerves.

'He had a sense for the occasion all of the time, and if it was a league game he wasn't too worried, but if it was a game in Croke Park in August... he'd rise to it instantly. He loved the big stage, and loved to be out there in the centre of that stage.

'And he was a powerful man. The worst rattle I got in all of my time playing for Galway was against him in an Allstars game in Chicago. He hit me accidently, and I went down like a tonne of bricks.

'He had amazing strength.'

They last met in the spring of 2017. Hayes asked his former teammate if he was ever going to put on any weight, or show even a few grey hairs? Tony took pride in announcing that he was only four pounds heavier than he had been on the morning of the 1988 All-Ireland final.

'Whether it was true or not,' recalls Hayes, '... he looked as fit as he had been back then.'

When he heard that Tony had suffered a heart attack, Conor Hayes put down his mobile phone. He did not want to examine in any detail what he had just been told by text message. He needed time. Then he got another text.

Hayes rang Pat Malone.

He knew Malone was closer to Tony and might know more. Hayes was told it did not look good. He still did not believe what he was being told.

'I did not think it possible,' he confesses.

At the beginning of 2017 a few of the lads from the All-Ireland winning teams of the 1980s had had a little chat amongst themselves. They agreed that the team's celebration weekend in 2012, when they were invited to Croke Park to celebrate their 25th anniversary as All-Ireland champions, was fine but that it might be good for the team to try it again. The great recession had not quite blown itself out by 2012. Times were still hard for most people.

Hayes and the others chatted about doing something special.

'When we had our 25th celebration in Croke Park well... it was a bad time for the country, and everyone was hurting a little bit. We were saying we should do something... one more time.'

They talked about the Camino de Santiago, for instance. The ancient six-weeks walk across the roof of Spain, following 'the way' of St James with thousands and thousands of other pilgrims.

'We talked about doing the last 100 miles of the Camino together... not the whole thing. You can meet in hotels anytime, and you can play golf anywhere, here in Ireland or in Spain, but it's still just a game of golf.

'Something special is what we talked about.

'But if we were doing that walk, well... it would be hard to imagine doing it now without Tony... without him out there leading the way.'

•••◆•••

TONY KEADY KNEW that his father's days were numbered.

He lived with that knowledge. He also hurled with the same knowledge, reminding himself on a regular basis that Jimmy Keady might never see him hurl again, or that Jimmy Keady might never again hear about the game his son had played in.

His father had been ill for so long.

'I knew he wasn't going to live too long,' Tony explained himself. 'Every day he was still alive was a bonus. It had been going on for so long, you just didn't know when the day would dawn.

'So, every match I played, I could feel it as a burden on my shoulders.'

The final game of hurling that Jimmy was told about was the 1985 All-Ireland hurling semi-final. Galway defeated Cork, against all the odds, on August 4 by 4-12 to 5-5 and just over two weeks later, on August 20, Tony's father died.

Tony, initially, did not want to hear anything about the distant possibility that he might play in the All-Ireland final against Offaly. He could not get his head around such a notion.

For so long, he had been waiting and preparing for the days that would follow the passing of his father and now that they had thundered down upon him, he felt floored. Completely. 'I could not get my head around hurling in the final,' he honestly confessed.

'I had no interest in it.'

The Galway lads called to his house.

They were there for him. As was his manager, Cyril Farrell. They all encouraged him to come back training. His mother joined the same chorus.

And Tony could hear his father's voice, and it was that voice that finally settled it. 'You were listening to them,' he reflected, 'but you were hurting so bad. But my father was mad for hurling and deep inside I knew that he'd want me to play... that he might not forgive me if I didn't. My mother kept saying it too.'

On the evening of his father's funeral Tony actually trained for the All-Ireland final, and on the field he could feel his father's presence more heavily and more supportive than ever before.

When Galway lost the 1985 final, Tony imagined Jimmy Keady being more heartbroken than anyone else in the whole county.

•••◆•••

WINNING CAME EASY enough to Tony Keady and his teammates, to begin with, in their teenage years. There were under-14, under-16, minor and under-21 championship medals earned with his club, and in 1983 he added a junior championship medal with Killimordaly. As adults, however, they quickly discovered that dues had to be earned the hardest way most often.

Killimordaly had to endure the heartache of back-to-back losses in the county senior final in 1984 and '85, before winning the big one at last in 1986 – same as Tony would have to endure a double setback with Galway on All-Ireland final day in 1985 and '86 before lifting the MacCarthy Cup in 1987.

Killimordaly would only win the one senior title.

They had lost finals in 1965, and again in 1970 and '76, before launching themselves at a senior title again a decade later. Castlegar beat them decisively by 3-10 to 0-11 in '84, and Turloughmore did do so handily 12 months later by 1-14 to 1-4, before Killimordaly turned the tables in 1986. They shot 17 points to Turloughmore's 2-7, and Tony and the lads would add a single Connacht medal to their meagre senior haul when they saw off Tooreen, 6-16 to 1-4.

On the national stage, long before he was part of Cyril Farrell's hunting party, he had quickly discovered that it was hard enough to reach a final, and then twice as difficult to win the thing. Granted he won his first All-Ireland medal with the Galway Vocational School team in 1980 when they saw off the challenge of Down, and the team retained their title the following year when Offaly were accounted for, but in 1980 he was also part of the Galway minor team that lost in the All-Ireland semi-final to Wexford after a replay, and in '81 Galway reached the minor decider and hit the ground running on the most prestigious Sunday of the whole year in Croke Park before being hauled back by Kilkenny.

THE MAROON NO.6 SHIRT was not Tony's exclusive property when he first stepped outside of his own county.

He wore No.11 and No.14.

He was centre-forward on the Galway team that met Wexford in the All-Ireland minor semi-final on August 3, 1980, and he scored three points to show that he was able to earn his keep amongst the forwards. However it was a game that Galway left behind them. They were nine points in front coming up to half-time thanks in the main to the heroics of Ollie Kilkenny, and six minutes into the second-half Tony clipped over a point to keep a healthy eight points margin between the teams.

'Galway will reflect on this result in the same vein as the fisherman who rued the one that got away,' reported Pat Roche in *The Irish Times*. *'... for in truth they seemed to have their place in the All-Ireland minor hurling final against Tipperary well and truly secured at different junctures of quite an amazing semi-final at Croke Park yesterday.'* Two points from John Codd had Wexford in front with time running down. Eanna Ryan came on and put Galway back in front, but Ted Morrissey had the final say for Wexford.

Galway 1-15, Wexford 0-18.

Three weeks later, Wexford had a three points lead at half-time (1-7 to 1-4) and they doubled that difference by the end (2-13 to 2-7). Codd, Morrissey and Martin Fitzhenry made the difference for the winners, and Tony only managed a single point against Wexford's No.6 Eamonn Cleary.

GALWAY WERE CROWNED All-Ireland Vocational Schools champions in 1980, which was some compensation for the disappointment against Wexford, and in the first week of May in '81 they retained their title when commanding it over Offaly by 1-11 to 1-5 in Thurles. Tony was in full-forward.

He slotted over one point, but in early August he was back at No.11 for the county minors when they met Clare in the All-Ireland semi-final in Croke Park and he cracked home a goal, and also slotted two points, in a 3-14 to 3-8 victory. Anthony Cunningham took the honours on the day with a return of 2-2, but Tony's hunger and swashbuckling demeanour singled him out as one of the architects of the victory.

Galway had two teams on the field on All-Ireland final day.

In the second game the seniors failed in the defence of the MacCarthy Cup when, in a hectic second-half, Johnny Flaherty secured Offaly's first title with a memorable goal. In the minor final Galway got off to a blistering start and had the sliothar in the Kilkenny net after just 20 seconds.

Galway led by 3-5 to 1-8 at half-time.

The teams were level by the 11th minute of the second-half. Tony hadn't scored in the first-half, and didn't manage to get his name onto one of Galway's four second-half points as a Ray Heffernan-inspired Kilkenny took greater, and greater, control of proceedings, finally winning by five points, 1-20 to 3-9.

Tony Keady won one All-Ireland final and lost one in 1981, and his career was at an interesting crossroads.

He was bound for a central role in the county defence, and two years later, with Pete Finnerty on one side of him and Ollie Kilkenny on the other, there was no mistaking a man who had found a place for himself on the field that looked his true home. In the No.6 shirt he was in control of his own destiny.

Manning the doorway of the Galway defence was a role he was born for, and he knew it.

THREE YEARS ON the county under-21 team continued Tony Keady's roller-coaster ride of thrills, and more spills.

Tony was now measuring himself against the greatest young hurlers in the country, and all of them from the traditional giants of the game. A Kevin

Hennessy point was just enough for Cork in a 0-12 to 0-11 win in the 1982 All-Ireland under-21 final, and Tony's last year on the team would also end in bitter disappointment but leave him with a taste of Tipperary as perhaps the ultimate opponents. Galway would lose the 1984 All-Ireland under-21 semi-final to Tipperary in Ennis by five points, 3-10 to 2-8, and the game really turned on a six pence at the start of the second-half when a Michael McGrath penalty was saved and, within a minute, a Colm Bonner clearance out of the Tipp defence somehow mystified Galway goalkeeper, Tommy Coen and ended in the net.

Tipperary had taken their revenge.

Because the previous year, in September of 1983, a serious rivalry first sparked when Galway got the better of Tipp in the under-21 final in Tullamore witnessed by over 6,000 spectators. It was a strange game. Tipperary failed to score at all in the opening half, as the esteemed GAA correspondent of *The Irish Times*, Paddy Downey explained in his match report the next morning.

'Galway had only three points to spare at the end of yesterday's keenly fought game, but they were worthy winners of a title which the county held previously in 1972 and 1978. Tipperary, who dominated the under-21 championship for three years up until 1982 had fancied their chances of regaining the trophy. They made their task a great deal harder, however, when failing to score in the first-half.

'Galway played with the aid of a strong wind in that period, but scored only five points. At the interval that lead did not look nearly enough to withstand a Tipperary rally, but as events transpired it proved to be ample.'

The Galway defence stood firm.

There was no budging, wind or no gale force wind, and Tommy Coen was in his very best form and pulled off two brilliant saves. He needed to be, because in the second-half the Tipp goalkeeper, Ken Hogan was bombing puckouts down upon the Galway defence.

By the end of the afternoon, Tony had the added pleasure of having outscored his opposite number in the blue and gold No.6 shirt. The young man in that shirt was Nicky English who, by the end of the decade, would be unanimously hailed as one of the most gifted forwards the country had ever seen. English didn't score; Tony grabbed a point.

It was a long and worrying second-half, that commenced with a Tipp goal to cut the deficit to two points.

'*Tipperary made a great start to the second-half when Martin McGrath's long free puck dropped in the square and Arthur Browne touched it through for a goal,*' continued Downey. '*That cut Galway's lead to two points and the possibility of victory for the Munster champions suddenly came alive. Twice subsequently Tipperary cut their arrears to a single point but Galway were equal to the challenge and their ability and determination pulled them out of trouble whenever the opposition threatened to level it.*

'*Galway took a lead of four points (0-11 to 1-4) with seven minutes to go but Tipperary again cut one point off that, and the game was once more in the melting pot. With less than a minute to go, however, Aidan Staunton scored the insurance point for Galway.*'

Galway 0-12, Tipperary 1-6.

Galway were All-Ireland champions, but 'The Galway and Tipperary Story' – the story that would command the attention of hurling supporters for the remainder of the decade – was only just beginning.

••• ◆ •••

BY THE CLOSE of 1985, Galway would announce themselves on the national stage and five of the team would collect Allstar awards. Seamus Coen, Sylvie Linnane, Pete Finnerty, Brendan Lynskey and Joe Cooney were voted the very best in their respective positions.

Although nominated alongside Pat Delaney of Offaly and Kilkenny's outstanding warhorse, Ger Henderson a similar acknowledgement was denied Tony. Delaney got the nod.

It was, after all, Offaly's year!

And it was against Offaly that Tony Keady, full of the joys of life, full of bravado also, and fearless, made his senior debut for Galway at the start of 1985.

The game was in Birr, and Galway travelled south as league leaders on February 10 of that year. It looked straightforward for the visitors, as the home team was without the services of Pat Carroll, Joe Dooley, Tom Connelly and Eugene Coughlan, but after a first-half in which the teams were level on three occasions, it was Offaly who struck for the finish line. They hit seven points to Galway's return of just two.

The game, effectively, was a shootout between Paddy Corrigan and Mick Haverty, and while the Galway free-taker was successful with eight out of his 10 attempts at goal from play and placed balls, Corrigan's tally reached nine points.

In *The Irish Independent*, Donal Carroll reported that the best team won, and only two men acquitted themselves as expected in the Galway defence. *'Galway will want to forget this game,'* wrote Carroll, *'and few of the team were outstanding except for their accurate free taker, Mick Haverty, and Michael McGrath in the forwards. Steve Mahon played soundly in centrefield but the backs, except for Tony Keady and Conor Hayes, were always under pressure.'*

Nevertheless, when the Galway team to face Cork in the All-Ireland semi-final was announced in late summer all of the national newspapermen noted in their opening paragraphs that Galway had taken a leap into the future by naming 'a whole new' half-back line.

Pete Finnerty, Tony Keady and Tony Kilkenny were in, and out were Steve Mahon, Michael Mooney and Ollie Kilkenny who had manned up in Galway's last competitive game in the Ford Trophy in May. Mahon was moved to midfield to partner team captain, Michael Connolly. Mooney was named on the bench, and Kilkenny was not considered because he had recently got married and had been missing from training for several weeks.

The biggest question mark placed against the new look half-back line landed above Tony's head, however.

In *The Irish Times*, Paddy Downey put down such a mark and then noted, *'Keady, a strong, talented player is not without senior experience, however. He played a few games for the county in the early part of the year and was at right half-back in the league semi-final against Clare and also in the Railway Cup final when an all-Galway side represented Connacht against Munster.'*

Tony was in against Cork and by the end of the afternoon of August 4, 1985 it would be noted by one respected national newspaperman that the reigning champs were left *'bedraggled, buffeted and bewildered.'*

Only 8,205 people turned up in GAA HQ to see what happened, though even half of them may have come in the hope that they were present for some historic occasion that might rival the 'Thunder and Lightning' All-Ireland final of 1939 when Kilkenny KO'd Cork in the most spectacular conditions. The first Sunday in August of 1985 promised the very worst of the Irish weather.

In *The Irish Press*, Peadar O'Brien left his readers in no doubt about just how treacherous the conditions facing Galway and Cork were. *'Croke Park, even with a generous coating of grass, was awash in places and players found it almost impossible to stop or turn suddenly without ending up on the sodden turf. Water squirted in all directions when players tried a first-time pull and yet, in spite of all that, the standard of play at times was remarkably good and a credit to all concerned.'*

Sean Kilfeather, in *The Irish Times*, was particularly taken by the balance and bravery of the Galway half-back line. *'The trio – Pete Finnerty, Tony Keady and Tony Kilkenny – were nothing short of superb. Their speed to the ball, their calmness under pressure, their use of the opportunities that came their way and above all their ceaseless covering for each other simply absorbed all that Cork could muster.'*

And that was the truth of it.

Cork lined out without the imperious Jimmy Barry Murphy, who had been injured in a club football match the week before, and only called him into action with 10 minutes remaining. Galway, in the meantime, had Brendan Lynskey who in the estimation of most of the gentlemen in the press box did 'the work of three.'

Galway would win.

They'd take the game by 4-12 to 5-5, an audacious nine-goal shootout in the spills of rain. Cork won the toss and decided to face the worst of the weather to begin with, and when they scored the first goal of the nine in the 10th minute, when John Fenton drove home from a penalty, they could be forgiven for thinking that their decision was quite smart. But Galway responded immediately when Noel Lane worked his magic and left Bernie Forde with the opportunity of connecting with the ball over his head and sending it past Ger Cunningham in the Cork goal.

Galway led 1-7 to 2-3 at half-time. When Joe Cooney dashed through a hesitant Cork defence to palm a second goal, and Lane and Forde tagged on points, it was 2-10 to 3-4 in Galway's favour, and the winners were about to produce their best hurling of the whole sodden day. A move involving Lane, Forde and Cooney ended with Lynskey netting, and it was 3-10 to 3-4.

Galway were well on their way to the All-Ireland final.

••• ◆ •••

FIVE WEEKS BEFORE his death, Tony looked back at that particular day against Cork in the company of John Harrington, a writer with *GAA.ie*, who was interviewing him in advance of his Legends Tour of Croke Park.

He noted that an extra special piece of history was made in the victory over Cork as it was decided that the Man of the Match award should be divided between three people.

'I was at the beginning of my career, and he was at the end of his,' he told Harrington, in reference to Tim Crowley. 'The 1985 semi-final was an awful wet day. I think the game was only on a minute and I went running for a ball but the two legs went from under me.

'Crowley rolled it up with one hand and threw it over the bar.

'Before I even got up off the ground I looked over to the sideline and thought... *they're probably making a little spot for me to sit down with them.*

'Two or three minutes after that another ball came down the middle and landed into a little slush in the ground. Myself and Crowley pulled around four or five times and all you could hear was the two hurls clashing and a big splash going up in the air every time.

'The ball never moved.

'So, I kind of said to myself... *I can compete with this lad!*

'That was progress as far as I was concerned.

'On the day Tony Kilkenny was wing back beside myself and Finnerty and they brought the three of us up to Micheal O'Muircheartaigh upstairs and gave three of us Man of the Match that day.

'I was only gone the 20 or thereabouts.

'It was huge.'

••• ◆ •••

'I COULD FEEL he was ready,' Cyril Farrell stresses still, almost three decades down the road. 'He had that thing about him... and he was stubborn on the field. Plus, of course, Tony was a solid hurler... a great hurler it turned out.'

It was Farrell, in his second coming as Galway team boss, who was unflinching in his decision to place the ultimate responsibility of the No.6 shirt with Tony. 'He had his three years with the under-21s and I knew we'd find out about him fast enough... and we did.'

Farrell was one of the youngest managers in the country when he guided Galway to their historic All-Ireland title in 1980. He was there in 1981 when Galway looked to retain the Liam MacCarthy Cup, but fell to a hungry and sometimes delerious Offaly, and in '82 when Galway collapsed at the semi-final stage it was time for Farrell to move on. Cyril Farrell, more than anybody, knew and felt the fickle nature of folk.

Farrell, the son of a farmer and publican, from Woodford, had hurled with Tommy Larkin's and helped them to one county title, and was working in Dublin when one of life's tragedies hauled him back home west for good. On a normal enough July day in 1968, Cyril travelled to the bog with his father.

Mick Regan was driving the tractor. Cyril was in the trailer with his uncle, Brian. His father was sitting on the mudguard, beside Mick, and they were passing a cigarette to one another when the tractor hit a bump on the road.

Before anyone knew it, Cyril's father had slipped down in front of the back wheel of the tractor. He was 53 years-old, and he died in front of Cyril.

Back home, Farrell signed on as a mature student at University College Galway. He would become a teacher, and eventually take up the post as school principal in St Raphael's College in Loughrea. But in UCG, surrounded by talented hurlers from all over Galway and far beyond, he had already began a life journey that would, speedily, present him as one of the smartest team managers in the country.

Farrell saw that the young Galway hurlers in the college were every bit as good, and just as ambitious, as any of the lads from other counties. On the field, together, he saw absolutely no difference between them, so how on earth had Galway become an outpost, serving the grand old game of hurling as a doormat more than a house of genuine dreams.

It was not something that could really be explained, or at all understood. Unless anyone chose to leaf through the game's history books, and trace a story of a county that had slowly, repeatedly, being beaten down. The 1950s had been cruel to Galway. The epic battle with Cork in 1953, the tough loss to Wexford in the '55 final, and the more disheartening day against Tipperary in the '58 decider. Then there was the 10-year experiment of including Galway in the Munster championship from 1959 that went perilously close to completely wiping Galway off the hurling map.

Cyril Farrell was 23 years-old, a young man with hopes he wished to firm up with hard work, when he was invited to take up a role with the county minor team. It was 1973. Sickening defeats of the past were old war stories, as far as Farrell was concerned. Before he got his hands on the senior team, he first of all guided the under-21s to an All-Ireland final in 1978 where they met Tipperary, drew with them, and went straight back out and defeated them in a replay.

Farrell had an exceptional faith in Galway's next generation, and when he viewed strapping young lads like Tony Keady, and saw how stubborn they were, arrogant as well, and solidly ambitious, right to their core, he knew that betting on them carried fewer risks than people around him might think.

At the same time, the people of Galway were especially gloomy.

The pages of *The Connacht Tribune* spoke up on their behalf in one edition in August of 1984. The previous Sunday Offaly had dispatched Galway in an All-Ireland semi-final and sent them home with a 14-point hiding (4-15 to 1-10) to think about through the winter.

GALWAY HURLING IS DEAD AND BURIED

That was the headline on Michael Glynn's report from Semple Stadium. Inside, Glynn wrote, *'Galway hurling died on Sunday – having been in a critical condition for some time. The passing away was relatively un-mourned, however, with the feeling persisting that the demise was partially self-inflicted.*

'Whatever the cause, there was more life in the proverbial doornail – and certainly that inanimate object has rarely endured a pounding of the type that Offaly doled out with such relish in Thurles on Sunday.'

Tom Rooney, on the same page, offered his thoughts under quite a different heading indeed.

NEW BREED OF HURLER IS NOW REQUIRED

'*The story of Galway hurling since the historic victory of 1980 is a sad one,*' wrote Rooney. '*That great day was the beginning of a deadly decline. It is time to use a more investigative criteria for selecting talent for the county. Even more important in today's competitive environment are individual qualities, such as application and character. The two qualities have been absent for a while in Galway teams.'*

John McIntyre, that same week, offered answers as well as asking questions, as he wrote of Galway's forthcoming All-Ireland under-21 semi-final against Tipperary when they would be defending their title.

He named young men.

Tommy Coen, Pete Finnerty and Tony Keady.

Michael Costello.

Michael Coleman, Michael McGrath and Eanna Ryan.

And Ollie Kilkenny and Sean Treacy.

The men in the newsroom in *The Connacht Tribune*, and the men standing in the middle of the floor in the Galway dressing room – Cyril Farrell and his selectors, Bernie O'Connor and Phelim Murphy – were on the same page in believing what needed to be done.

It could not be done slowly.

••••◆••••

SYLVIE LINNANE HAD told Cyril Farrell that he was the best wing-back that Farrell had in the county.

He told the manager this more than once.

'I need you to be the best corner-back,' Farrell replied.

More than once.

Farrell sensed a defence in the making. A half-back line of Pete Finnerty, Tony Keady and Gerry McInerney was still a little way off, but a full-back threesome of Sylvie Linnane, Conor Hayes and Ollie Kilkenny was under his nose.

The league campaign would end unceremoniously in 1985, with Clare on a bit of a gallop and defeating Galway by six points. In May, in the final of the Ford Trophy, a newly titled version of the Centenary Cup from 1984, and played on an open draw basis, Tipperary had taken Galway out of it in the final by three points, 1-13 to 1-10. In that game, Farrell realised he should fast-track the making of a whole new half-back line.

It was now September of '85, and the last two were standing in front of the whole country, Galway and Offaly.

Glorious September.

And disastrous September, possibly?

The face of the Galway team had changed, though there remained a strain from 1980 still. Seven of the men who won All-Ireland medals that year were to be found – Hayes and Sylvie, Michael Connolly, Mahon, Molloy, Forde and Lane!

Talking to the media in advance of the game, Farrell was straight-up and also philosophical about past and present.

Cyril Farrell: We brought in a panel of players and started training with the immediate objective of staying in the first division of the National League. We believed we had the nucleus of a good team, if we could get the commitment of the players and could pull it together properly. We got that commitment. After that it was up to us to do our job... I believe it is the job of every man in charge to make every player believe he's the best... even if he's not.

(August 31, 1985)

•••◆•••

OFFALY HAD TORN Galway apart in the semi-final in 1984, and the previous February they had enjoyed a seven-point victory over Farrell's men in the league. Galway were a team in the making. Offaly, on the other hand, was made up of grizzled, hardened tradesmen and a few geniuses. And Offaly were just as hungry as Galway.

They held all the natural advantages.

Galway, really, held none.

Offaly, in the Leinster semi-final, had fought back from nine points down to force a replay with Kilkenny, and they had won that replay by six points. They had 13 points to spare over Laois in the provincial final. They had one All-Ireland title and four Leinster titles under their belt, and unlike Galway they believed that they were fully deserving of the next All-Ireland title before, perhaps, resting on their laurels.

For some season, however, the men in the newspaper business were calling

Galway as overwhelming favourites.

That may have made total sense to the likes of Tony Keady, as one of eight newcomers only dying to get out there and win the damn thing, but to Farrell it was worrying.

In the 1985 All-Ireland final, Galway were indeed fearless. Everyone knew they would be, except their display was laced with fearlessness and some foolishness. They would shoot 20 wides, 13 of them in a wild first-half at the end of which they trailed by 1-6 to 0-7.

Offaly would win it, 2-11 to 1-12.

The crucial goal for Offaly came shortly after the restart when a Pat Cleary shot actually entered the net off the knee of Sylvie Linnane. Galway were gracious in defeat, even though there was another goal, that might have been, but wasn't given as a goal, to talk about.

That ghost of a goal that might have overturned Offaly's two-point winning margin was the talking point for the next 24 hours.

Tony Keady would talk about it so many years later, but would be unable to shine any more light on it naturally. He had marked Brendan Bermingham. His man had got just a single point on him. Tony had been steady-to-good all through his first All-Ireland final, no more.

A ghost goal?

'You don't think about those things for too long,' Tony explained. 'I was a long way away from what happened anyway, but I honestly believe you win games that you really deserve to win... and the others you lose, and nobody wants to hear you talk about those for too long. There's an awful lot of teams who could talk about games and finals they should have won...

'Who'd want to listen to them?'

Interestingly, at the same time, the umpire on duty at the Railway end of the ground, 43 year-old Michael Collins from Tipperary town, was willing to discuss what he saw. Collins admitted to journalists the next day that the ball did cross the Offaly goal-line (as RTE's film of the ghost goal also clearly shows) but asserted that PJ Molloy was inside the small square at the same time.

Galway were one point behind coming up to the end of the third quarter. Joe Cooney sent the ball into the Offaly goalmouth. It was diverted by Aiden

Fogarty, the Offaly right full-back and the spinning ball hit the roof of the net before dropping and landing one foot inside the goal-line, before spinning back out into play. At that point, Offaly captain Pat Fleury struck it out of his way for a '70'.

Michael Collins: I was watching Molloy and he was definitely inside the square. I had my mind made up at that stage that even if the ball went in, I certainly would not allow a goal. Perhaps I should have consulted the referee, but there was no doubt in my mind that it was not a goal.

(September 3, 1985)

THE REFEREE GEORGE Ryan from Tipperary admitted that he did not know what had happened until he was informed by his umpire after the game. He told newspapermen at the luncheon for both teams the day after the final that he could not comment any further on what happened, except to add that if his umpire had informed him as he saw it, then he would have awarded a free out to Offaly. He also mentioned that Michael Collins was one of his best umpires, and had been part of his 'team' for 10 years.

Cyril Farrell: This sort of thing is part of the fortunes of fast field games. We hold no grudges. We were well on top in the first-half and overall we had a 60:40 share of the play, but we did not put away our chances. Of course, we got none of the lucky breaks either.

(September 3, 1985)

CHAPTER 2

1986

IT WOULD BEGIN and it would end as a year of reflection. On hurling, and on life itself, and what it was all about?

In March of 1986, the outstanding Offaly hurler, Pat Carroll passed away after fighting for his life for seven months. Carroll had played in all of Offaly's games in 1985, but had to pull out of the team's preparations for the All-Ireland final because he was suffering from severe headaches.

The day after he died, the hurling community mourned, but immediately the games continued and Galway suited themselves up in the green of Connacht and gave Munster something of a roasting in the Railway Cup final in Duggan Park in Ballinasloe in front of a mainly home crowd of 6,300 spectators.

Galway were winning games through the spring, including a four-point defeat of Offaly in Birr that was a small measure of revenge for the All-Ireland final loss of the previous September. A very small measure. But the humbling of Munster was the fourth time in seven seasons that Connacht had won the Railway Cup, and by beating Offaly, Dublin (0-16 to 1-9), Cork (0-25 to 0-10), Laois (3-6 to 0-8), Clare (0-12 to 0-5), and Wexford in the league semi-final after a replay (3-11 to 2-5) a place had been earned in the league final.

But Galway would be well beaten in the 1986 league final by Kilkenny, 2-10 to 2-6, a second successive loss to the Cats who had also won an earlier league battle by 2-9 to 0-9.

And Galway would work their way through the summer of 1986 – one that was wet, wet, wet – before also losing to a Cork team whom they were informed by everyone they should defeat in the 1986 All-Ireland final.

Losses in big games were mounting up into quite an untidy pile of disappointment and remorse.

Tony, by the very end of the year, had his doubts about what he was doing. A great man like Pat Carroll had won an All-Ireland, and then passed away so quickly. Other men could spend all of their lives trying and failing to win an All-Ireland medal. What was it all about?

Tony also had one eye on his brother in the United States. Noel Keady was running his own successful construction company in Boston, and Tony found himself weighing up all of the hard work on the hurling field versus lots of hard work in the building trade, and fun and total freedom from grave disappointments.

A life in Galway V's a life in Boston?

'There was good money to be made in America,' he later explained, when journeying back to his state of mind at the close of 1986. 'I was toying with the idea of going over to Noel.

'All I had won at that stage was a *Connacht Tribune* bicycle, a Vocational School and an All-Ireland under-21. Who remembers them?

'It was nothing.

'You're wondering if you have the time to put in another year and, maybe, get no result at the end of it again?

'Noel had a serious set-up over there... I was very tempted.'

Tony decided to stay put and soldier on with Cyril Farrell and his team in 1987, but the notion of going to America was never high-shelved and layered in dust.

America stayed alive.

TONY KEADY MISSED 10 weeks during the spring of 1986 because of a nasty leg injury, and only got back onto the field when nearly everything was going wrong in the league final on a sodden pitch that was cutting up, but one which Kilkenny seemed to find not at all troublesome.

Pearse Piggott was in at centre-back for the team in Tony's absence, and he had acquitted himself superbly in the two semi-final games against Wexford, but even though Tony had only returned to training a week earlier Cyril Farrell knew that he had no choice but to throw him into it at half-time. At that stage Kilkenny led 2-4 to 1-2, their goals coming from Christy Heffernan and Liam Fennelly inside the opening 14 minutes. Galway had failed to score between PJ Molloy's point in the first minute and Noel Lane's point in the 28th minute. Tony got the team to respond.

'*Keady shored up the half-back line,*' reported Peadar O'Brien in *The Irish Press*. '*He solved the problem in defence, and the team really came alive for the first time when Joe Cooney moved to midfield where he proved to be an outstanding figure for the rest of the game.*'

Galway scored one goal and three points between the 42nd and 51st minutes, and the Kilkenny advantage was brought back to one. But it was stretched back to four by the final whistle.

FARRELL AND HIS trusted sideline lieutenants believed they needed to give their team some added advantage. Before Galway met Kerry in Ennis, in the All-Ireland quarter-final on July 19, they had hatched a fairly elaborate plan. They needed it to be all mapped out and wrinkle free before they met Kilkenny, for a third time, in the semi-final on August 10.

Brendan Lynskey and Steve Mahon had been in the middle of the field against Kilkenny in the league final, but Ger Fennelly had been magnificent and cleaned them out. Farrell knew that Mahon was not a classic man-marker, but liked to be on the ball, and he fully understood that Lynskey was most effective for the team when he was making his surging runs forward.

Farrell was not going to play two midfielders against Kilkenny.

Neither was he going to have three half-forwards and three full-forwards, but he was going to make maximum use of Piggott and Tony Kilkenny.

With Finnerty, Keady and McInerney in his half-back line, the Galway manager knew that he had options. Those three were the key. If they commanded their line, then everything else would work simply, if not brilliantly.

Farrell decided to drop Ollie Kilkenny back to the full-back line, and he decided to push Tony Kilkenny up to midfield. Tony Kilkenny and Piggott would play alongside Steve Mahon in the middle of the field. Anthony Cunningham, Lynskey and Martin Naughton would form a strong running half-forward line. And, inside them, there would only be Joe Cooney and Noel Lane.

Galway would not play 2-3-3 against Kilkenny.

Farrell was set on playing the All-Ireland semi-final with an adventurous 3-3-2 formation. There would be great strength and lots of bodies in the centre of the field. And there would be plenty of room in Kilkenny's half for the likes of Cunningham and Naughton, and Cooney when he drifted out, to use their explosive speed to maximum advantage.

However, when he unveiled his plan to his team in Kenny Park in Athenry Farrell's players, especially his older crew, hated it.

Farrell huddled his lads around him in one of the very small dressing-rooms and went through every morsel of the plan. At the back of his head he knew that he had no choice but to try something new. Kilkenny had an iron grip on Galway in All-Ireland semi-finals, leading 14-5 in victories. They'd also taken Galway in the All-Ireland finals in 1975 and '79.

Cyril Farrell: All our training has been geared towards playing Kilkenny. We said in the dressing-room in Thurles after they beat us in the league final that we would be playing them in the semi-final and that has come true. Now it's a matter of whether or not we are good enough. What previous Galway teams did against Kilkenny was their business. If they let themselves think that Kilkenny were always better that was their mistake. I can tell you that this team will not do that.'

(August 10, 1986)

THE PLAN WAS exciting, but it would surely fall apart if the Galway half-back line did not present itself as the obstinate, strong-willed outer wall of a fortress.

More than once, Tony kidded around when talking about his 'working relationship' with Finnerty and McInerney. 'When we're together and there's people around,' he would recall years later, 'I like to have the banter, and I always say to the two boys that the basis to a good half-back line is to have a really great centre-back.

'I don't have to tell you what happens when I say that!

'To be honest, people will always say to a centre-back that when a ball is coming down on a wing-back, cover in behind.

'But I don't believe I ever had to do that.

'And I'll tell you, if I had... I would have been told where to go!

'To have those two beside you was great. You'd hate when you'd miss a match or one of them would miss a match... and the chain would be broken.

'They were two serious operators... no doubt.'

Though Tony's respect for those he took the field with was not at all limited to men who wore jerseys between No.1 and No.7. 'If you looked at our forwards, and you were the manager, you couldn't come to terms with taking any of them off... if they were playing badly.

'All you had to do was move them... that was it.

'Lynskey, Cooney, Hopper, Naughton, Anthony Cunningham and Eanna Ryan... they were just super. You could play them from midfield in anywhere. They were a special bunch to be hitting a ball down to...

'I can tell you!'

But as the All-Ireland semi-final loomed, commentators were looking at Tony Keady especially, and his impending battle with Kilkenny's giant from the village of Glenmore, Christy Heffernan. It was Heffernan who had broken Galway to begin with in the league final with a goal.

Heffernan was noted as a full-forward, but once those big boots of his started moving he could stomp on a defender in any part of the field. In *The Irish Times*, Paddy Downey singled out this match-up as central to the outcome of the 1986 All-Ireland semi-final.

'With Peter Finnerty and Tony Keady back to full fitness, and with Gerry McInerney fitting in splendidly at left half-back, this line can now be regarded as Galway's strong point. Kilkenny persist with Christy Heffernan at centre half-forward and in doing so may be suiting Galway's purposes. Heffernan is a deadly finisher near goal but has yet to prove himself mobile enough for the 'forty'. Keady will give

him very little room to line up his shots and if he can be held, Kilkenny's ace may be
trumped. One cannot see Heffernan playing in this position for the full 70 minutes.'

THE PLAN WORKED.

Galway 4-12, Kilkenny 0-13.

As long as he remained on Tony, Christy Heffernan did not score – and he
left the field with nothing to his name.

'Kilkenny were not merely beaten by 11 points,' wrote Donal Keenan in *The*
Irish Independent, '... they were outhurled, out-manoeuvered and overrun by a
Galway team that was brimming over with running and hurling from start to finish.'

Kilkenny, from the beginning, looked baffled.

By the 21st minute, they had called ashore their teak-tough defender
Paddy Prendergast and replaced him with John Mulcahy, a forward, in a
frantic bid to undo damage that was long done. The Cats defence was indeed
overrun. Their vaunted midfield flattened.

'Full-back Conor Hayes was superb,' continued *The Irish Independent's* GAA
correspondent, *'... Tony Keady brilliant, and left half-back Gerry McInerney simply*
awe-inspiring.'

In the eight minute, Joe Cooney placed Noel Lane and the Galway captain
palmed the ball to the net. It was 1-5 to 0-5 after 26 minutes, but Galway were
only getting into their stride, as Kilkenny remained wobbling. Cooney and
Anthony Cunningham combined magnificently for goal No.2. It was 2-7 to
0-5 at half-time. Everyone expected Kilkenny to clear their heads at half-time.
It didn't happen. Cooney pounced for a goal, and Naughton raced down the
right and found Cooney inside for goal No.4.

Galway were back in an All-Ireland final, and as Cork had made such a
meal of getting over Antrim in the other semi-final – scoring seven goals, but
allowing their opponents to tot up 1-24 – there was a genuine belief among
most neutral GAA fans that 1986 was destined to belong to Farrell and Co.

It wasn't the case, of course, and if Galway thought that life at the top was
not hard enough, there was some other news on the same weekend as their
defeat of Kilkenny which would make the whole business of winning All-
Ireland titles, and retaining them, twice as difficult.

Michael 'Babs' Keating was named as the new Tipperary hurling boss, succeeding Tony Wall, and the star forward from the 1960s and 70s would have two other healthy names from Tipp's past, Donie Nealon and Theo English, alongside him as he plotted the Premier County's fast return to greatness.

CORK DELIGHTED IN showcasing a virtual 'hospital ward' in the run-in to the All-Ireland final.

Already, they had travelled an undistinguished route to the decider. They beat a weak Waterford team in their first game in Munster. They took down Clare in the provincial final, no big deal! And they only beat poor little Antrim by five points in the All-Ireland semi-final. Their chances of winning a 26th All-Ireland title was further dimmed by an injury crisis, they happily announced.

They had definitely lost two of their toughest defenders, Dermot MacCurtain and John Hodgkins, but the fitness of their right full-back Pat Hartnett was also suppose to be in doubt. Left full-back Johnny Crowley had a thigh strain that was not going away. Midfielder John Fenton was nursing a twisted ankle.

Cork were also quick to admit that their centre-back, Richard Browne had not fully settled into his position, and that they might have to gamble on 20 year-old Teddy McCarthy, better known as a footballer, in the forward division.

But, with his back up against a wall, Cork team boss Johnny Clifford could not resist spelling out a warning.

Johnny Clifford: I know they have been criticised. I know they have been written off in some quarters because of those championship displays but take my advice, don't ever write off a Cork team. How can you write off a team that had 25 All-Ireland medals between them? How can you write off a team many of whom have been involved in three All-Ireland finals over the last four years? I think all of the hard work has been done. It is only a matter of waiting, sharpening our skills and learning how to be mentally prepared for the big one.

(September 4, 1986)

Conor Hayes: It's time we learned to be favourites. We have often in the past been underdogs and that didn't seem to help us either. Let's be frank about it... we just could not avoid becoming favourites for this year's All-Ireland final after the way we disposed of Kilkenny in Thurles. That was the finest display given by a Galway team since I first put on the jersey in senior. It would be a shame if we failed now.

(September 7, 1986)

Con Houlihan: Last year's semi-final remains a vivid memory, the conditions couldn't have been worse – but Galway hurled as if on a perfect sod. And several virtually unknown young players confounded their far more experienced opponents. It was the day of the raindance kids. Yesterday produced a game even more astonishing – not because Galway won but because they won by such a margin. The promise shown in last year's semi-final looks like being fulfilled.

(Evening Press, August 11, 1986)

Jimmy Barry Murphy: Even locally there are many who do not give us a chance. This is not surprising when you consider how Galway put out Kilkenny and how we performed against Antrim. Galway were not in the least flattered by the size of their victory. They ran at Kilkenny in the most confident fashion and exposed weaknesses in defence. I accept that we will have to produce a really top class performance on the day if we are to defeat them.

(August 31, 1986)

AND THEN THE game began.

In the 1986 All-Ireland final, Tony Keady would strike one of the biggest totals of his career, slapping over four frees and also landing a mighty '70' – and that left him one point better off than his man, Tomas Mulcahy who finished the game with 1-1. However, there was no satisfaction in coming out on top in such a 'miniature' contest.

Galway spent the afternoon chasing, not a good thing to be doing on All-

Ireland final day. They closed a six-point gap to draw level, 0-10 to 2-4, late in the first-half, but even at that stage it was obvious that the Cork management team had done their homework, and had done so late into many nights breaking down the manner of Galway's semi-final victory over Kilkenny.

Fenton and Kevin Hennessy scored the first two goals for the winners, and the pressure on the Galway defence, with Ger Cunningham's booming puck-outs clearing the heads of the Galway half-backs on occasions, never relented.

Meanwhile, at the other end, deep in the Cork defence, Johnny Crowley stayed in his corner and was not tempted to travel down the field. In this eventuality – if Clifford had told Crowley to stay put – then Farrell had told his men to run with the ball. Instead, ball after ball appeared to land in Crowley's lonesome corner, and Crowley was named Man of the Match on the evening of the All-Ireland final.

It ended 4-13 to 2-15.

Cork's 26th glorious title.

And feeling heartbroken for his players, Cyril Farrell found himself speaking out publicly at the mistreatment of some of them, and in particular Brendan Lynskey. Farrell was stinging in his criticism of Dublin referee, John F Bailey.

When he was subsequently called in front of the Games Administration Committee to explain himself, and perhaps suggest that he had been misquoted, Farrell stood his ground. He stood over everything he had said.

He got slapped with a two months suspension.

Dermot MacCurtain: We were in a bit of bother just before half-time, and for a while after it, but the teamwork was great. The great free-taking of Tony Keady gave us trouble. He was dangerous from frees everywhere. Pete Finnerty had a marvellous match and our half-forwards had to fight very hard for what they got. But they never gave up. They kept on putting the pressure on Galway. I feel sorrow for Galway. They have contributed so much to hurling and haven't won what they have deserved, but we never apologise for beating them. They wouldn't thank us for that.'

(September 8, 1986)

··· ◆ ···

TOMAS MULCAHY WAS under strict orders on the afternoons of the 1986 and 1990 All-Ireland finals. Johnny Clifford did not suffer fools, and was old school and clear-headed about what he wanted done. Equally, four years later the Canon, Fr Michael O'Brien was not a man who liked to have his orders ignored either.

Clifford, a powerful Glen Rovers man, only won one All-Ireland senior medal on the field, and had his career cut short by injury, but on three occasions in the 1980s and 90s he took up the job of managing the Cork senior team.

Fr Michael O'Brien was a man who lived and breathed hurling at college and county level. He had coached Farranferris to five Dr Harty Cup wins between 1969 and '74, and he led UCC to eight consecutive Fitzgibbon Cup titles in the 1980s, and was also in the background for two more victories in 1990 and '91. He was a busy man in 1990.

The Canon had co-managed Cork to their 1984 All-Ireland win alongside Justin McCarthy. In 1990 the Cork team boss had his eye on Tony Keady in particular. Just like Clifford had four years earlier.

'Tony was their lynchpin,' explains Mulcahy, '... and in 1986 I was under orders to stop him from getting free pucks and driving the ball down to our end of the field. I had to stop him dominating the game, and making inroads... and it was the same for Teddy McCarthy on Gerry McInerney.

'Teddy was there to stop McInerney from making those surging runs.

'The ball was being pucked down on top of myself and Tony, and I was trying to belt it on... but he'd put his hand up and pluck it out of the sky now and then. He had a mighty catch.'

Tomas Mulcahy, even though he did not know Tony personally and had met him seldom enough after each had retired, was present to bid a final sad farewell to a Galway warrior – a warrior he had met in armed combat.

'We had our words on the field with one another over the years... tough words most of the time, but when we finished up playing that was all forgotten about, but I didn't know enough about Tony. When I came up for his removal I heard a lot more about him.'

The 1986 All-Ireland final was the first time they went head-to-head with the whole country watching.

'When you look back on that Galway team, you first of all see the half-back line they had... because it probably best represented the strength of the team as a whole and characterised that power in the team.

'It was a brilliant team, but the half-back line was very dominant, and that is a thing that is key on all the great teams down through the years

'In '86 we had Tony O'Sullivan and Teddy McCarthy with me on the half-forward line, and we had Jimmy Barry Murphy and Kevin Hennessy and John Fitzgibbon inside... so we had a strong forward line out against that Galway defence. It was incredible how intense the whole game was.

'Our manager, Johnny Clifford was old school in his style of management and tactics, and my job that day was to keep the ball moving on the ground and get it into the inside line.'

Tomas Mulcahy does himself an injustice in that summation, because he was also a man to win the ball and take on his man, and surge forward towards goal. Something he did in the 1986 final. Actually the goal he scored in that final was judged Goal of the Year, though Mulcahy asks for that not to be mentioned.

'I scored a goal in '86... when I finally caught one ball over Tony's head.

'I raced inside, and I did over-carry the ball on the way... but what was I to do... I wasn't going to ask the referee if it was okay to over carry it?

'We had heard all about Galway's win over Kilkenny. To be fair, Johnny Clifford knew what he needed to do. He knew Galway would only play two men on the inside line against us.

'Johnny insisted on our backs staying where they were.

'Because of that, the ball was coming straight back out from our defence... from Ger Cunningham and Johnny Crowley. We were seeing a lot more ball coming down upon us in the half-forward line.

'As I say, it was an intense game, with open style hurling and free style hurling... and no one was taking a step back on either team.

'I didn't think Tony was the quickest on his feet, but his brain was amazing and his reading of the game was brilliant. He always knew where to be. And he could strike the ball off his left and his right... and the left was nearly as powerful as the right.

'At the same time, he also kept everyone around him on their toes... Finnerty and McInerney.'

Mulcahy fast-forwards to 1990.

'We had a bit of a spat in 1990 when I scored a goal.

'A lot of people have asked me over the years what we said to one another, and I always shrug it off and tell them... "Ah, we just said we'd meet for a drink when it was all over."

'But we did have words, and because we were at it hammer and tongs, and breaking hurleys, and not stopping at one another... there were always going to be a few words.'

Mulcahy had started the 1990 final in the corner. He had Ollie Kilkenny on him, but Cork were struggling at half-time, and continued to play second fiddle at the start of the second-half.

'Ten minutes into the second-half we were well behind, and switches were made. The Canon had been shouting and roaring at us in the dressing room.

'Three boys were brought into the showers and had iced buckets of cold water poured over them. The Canon was telling us we had 35 minutes to rectify things... and he said only three of us were worth our salt in the first half.'

It was at that point that Kevin Hennessy decided to cut through the ice in the Cork dressing-room and tongue in cheek ask the Canon... 'Who are the other two?'

'Kevin wasn't going that well himself,' continues Mulcahy, 'So it was a brave thing to say... but that was Kevin for you.

'During the second-half a ball came down... and it broke and I reacted faster than Tony. I soloed through, but I got a shoulder from someone as I was striking it... and I hit the side netting.

'I came running back out to my position and was met by Tony, who gave me an unmerciful shoulder, and he shouted at me... "Mul... you must have thought it was '86 all over again?"

'He was talking about that goal I had scored against him.'

Mulcahy shouldered Tony in reply.

And they went at it again.

'A couple of minutes later, the ball broke and I got through... and I scored a goal, and when I landed back out with him on the forty I could not stop myself. I had to say it to him... "Sorry Tony... it's '86 all over again!"

'But that's the banter you always have... the same stuff you can laugh about when you meet up years later. The thing about Tony Keady was... he was able to give it, and he was able to take it.

'Tony knew how the game was played... the physical side of it all and the mental stuff players try on one another in order to get into each other's heads.'

As Tomas Mulcahy joined people, and former hurlers, from all over the country at the long goodbye to a legend, he learned just how adept Tony had been at both sides of the game. After Tony's removal, he found himself in a pub having a coffee with Tony's old teammates, and listening to their stories, and sharing their laughter at how Tony responded to one young pup of a Galway hurler who had once dared to ask him why there was no hair on his chest?

'Young fella,' Tony responded, '...do you not know that hair never grows on steel!' With his own, and with opponents, Tony knew no mercy at times.

Mulcahy recounts another story he heard that same day.

'I was told in one game that he shouted over to Finnerty, who was totally decimating his man at the time.

'Tony shouted... "Horse... you need a hand over there?"

'Finnerty wasn't sure what he had heard, or why Tony was offering him any help and he shouted back... "What are you talking about... who are you talking to?"

'Looking directly at Finnerty's opponent, Tony replied... "I'm not talking to you Finnerty... I'm talking to that horse beside you!" '

•••◆•••

THE DEVASTATION AT losing two All-Ireland finals in-a-row, could only have been lessened, and finally calmed, by something magical and personal.

In November, Tony and Killimordaly won the Galway senior title for the first time. It was magical. It was personal.

And the year was saved from complete ruin.

Tony played a starring role in guiding his club to a 0-17 to 2-7 win over the holders, Turloughmore, in front of over 10,000 spectators in Ballinasloe.

Killimordaly showed patience and a surprisingly high level of self-belief in how they measured their use of the ball and worked, and worked and worked, for clearcut scoring opportunities. They had only scored eight times in their semi-final win over Athenry – three goals and five points – but in the final they doubled that total by being on target 17 times..

Eanna Ryan outshone Tony in the historic day for the men in the green and white hoops, appearing in the No.7 shirt, but thereafter deciding that the whole field was his kingdom. RTE commentator and local writer, Jim Carney was present to catch the tight closing sequence.

'*With nine minutes to go Frank Burke doubled on a loose ball for his second goal and suddenly the fat was in the fire again,*' wrote Carney in *The Tuan Herald*. '*... but after Turlough keeper Michael Shaughnessy fumbled a clearance Killimordaly forced a free and Haverty sent it over.*

'*Gerry Burke's confidence had been shaken by a couple of missed frees, and he shied away from going for a goal with a late effort from the right but at that stage anyway Killimordaly had one hand on the cup and the full-backs Tommy Skehill and Michael Earls and namesake Pat Earls were in no mood to allow Frank Burke in for his hat-trick. Michael Earls made one mighty catch in front of the goal and came out with the ball to swell the hearts of his supporters and when referee Seamus Brennan's final whistle sounded a tidal wave of emotion and relief swept over Duggan Park.*

'*If Eanna Ryan and Michael Earls starred for the winners, centre-back Tony Keady also put in a superlative second-half during which he struck two frees that reminded us of those prodigious efforts in the All-Ireland final.*'

In The *Connacht Tribune*, Francis Farragher wrote, '*There were some memorable moments of inspiration in those closing minutes with centre-back Tony Keady turning in a rousing finish highlighted by one tremendous burst upfield when he stormed through a 'meitheal' of Turlough players, before being given a free.*'

Killimordaly, at last, had lifted the big one in Galway club hurling, and they did so after twice in succession trooping home on county final day with their tails between their legs.

Basking in glory locally, Tony Keady and Eanna Ryan understood better than anyone else on the Galway team what one more outrageous effort might unearth on the national stage.

Even if one more year appeared as imposing as a flight to the moon.

LEGEND

CHAPTER 3

1987

BRENDAN LYNSKEY HEARD what Cyril Farrell was asking him, but it didn't make any sense at the same time.

Lynskey was asked to find Tony Keady.

Find him, and have a word with him, and maybe look after him. Help him? Farrell was in full flow. It was very early in 1985, the start of the season, and Farrell was back in charge and had asked Lynskey to rejoin the Galway senior squad.

Lynskey was happy to do so.

'I was working for Dublin Gas. Cyril told me he was going back in, and that he was picking a new panel... and he was going to do this and do that. He asked me if I would come back in?

'I had been dropped in 1983-84 from the panel.

'I was keen to get back in. There were still a good few fellas from the 1980 team there, and I had been on and off the panel for a while... and I felt that I wanted another go at it. I wanted to win an All-Ireland like them.

'Then he rang me again... and he told me that Tony Keady was in Rathmines working for Bank of Ireland.

'He told me that Tony was staying in a bedsit.

'That he knew nobody.

'But Cyril had no more information than that... not where Tony was living or what branch of the bank he was working in. I told him he needed to get me more information.

'I asked him how did he expect me to find Tony?

'This is Dublin, I told him... I can't be just driving up and down the streets looking for the man.'

Farrell asked if Lynskey had room where he was living for Tony?

Lynskey was living in 102 Phibsboro Road, in his brother's house, and he assured Farrell there was room for Tony there.

'I did not know Tony very well before then,' Lynskey continues. 'I had seen him and heard of him, but I had never spoken to him. But Farrell told me that he was bringing Tony onto the panel... that Tony was the coming No.6 for the county.

'Farrell came back with more information for me.

'And I went out to meet Tony, but I did not know how to approach the conversation. Farrell had said nothing to him, and I didn't know anything about Tony's situation... he could have been living with someone for all I knew.'

But Tony was happy to move across the city, to the northside, and he moved into No.102 and for the next four years, from 1985 till '89, Tony Keady and Brendan Lynskey were inseparable.

They became teammates

Best friends.

A pairing within an All-Ireland winning team that appeared to be a law unto itself at times. And they were happy for the media to portray them as such.

They slept in two single beds in the one room in No.102.

And in No.102 they ate, and they laughed at the notion that the pair of them were the two wild, lawless men on the Galway team. When they finished laughing, most often they would leave No.102 and go out for quiet, secret training sessions together.

There was a seven-year age gap between the two of them but Lynskey happily remembers... 'We got on from day one!'

'We built up a great relationship very quickly... but that was not hard in those days. We'd be travelling 26 and 27 nights... in-a-row sometimes... down to training in Galway. It was intense early season stuff... and we'd be travelling through all of those towns and villages that nobody has to pass through anymore because of the motorways.

'But, back then, we'd be on the road down to Galway for four hours... Lucan, Leixlip, Maynooth, Enfield, Kinnegad... Moate and Ballinasloe... and there'd still be another hour to Athenry.

'It was the guts of a nine-hour journey, up and back...leaving work at 3.0 in the middle of the day to be down there for 7.0... and getting home at 2.0 in the morning. And back to work for 8.0 or 9.0 the next morning.

'And then the same thing again.'

Behind everything, Brendan Lynskey is at pains insisting that Tony Keady was a true professional. Like everyone else on the Galway panel he would see Tony's 'divil may care' character.

But, back in No.102, Lynskey might be sitting there and Tony would tell him to throw on a tracksuit, and the next thing the two of them would be over in the Phoenix Park doing a few rounds.

'We did not have the money to drink in those times,' Lynskey continues, '... nobody had. Going for a run was free of charge.

'After the semi-final in '87 we went out and trained for two hours on our own. On wet days we'd run on the roads instead of the park... head down to Griffith Avenue... by the Skylon Hotel... right and onto Whitworth Road, and back to Phibsboro Road and No.102... a good run.

'We'd be running on the footpaths and people all around and nobody taking a blind bit of notice of the two of us.

'I was lucky in those days. My boss was Tony O'Sullivan, and by the name you can guess he was a good Corkman and a great GAA man. He was so good to me and gave me all the time off I needed. Tony was lucky with his boss too. There was no pressure put on the pair of us at work.

'We were blessed that way.

'Tony had that serious side that people did not know about. But I saw it... and I saw how that suited him. He'd lead people down the garden path... right until he pulled on the jersey.

'He could make the ball talk... in the same way that Joe Cooney could make it talk. I'd have to work twice as hard as him to be anything like that, and still not get there.'

One night before the 1988 All-Ireland final, Cyril Farrell was told that the Dublin pair were out drinking, that they were in the Merchant pub.

It was a Thursday night that Lynskey and Keady were supposed to be risking everything for a few pints, but Lynskey explains that that same evening they did not even manage to get back to Dublin until the earliest hours of the morning.

'We should have been back in Dublin that night, but on the way back we were going through Moate and Tony was driving... his yellow Kadett, and he tells me something's wrong with his car.

No power, Tony announced.

The car stopped.

There was no restarting it

'I looked over at him and said... "No petrol, Tony."

'We walked to Kilbeggan... Johnny Carroll had a petrol station there. Johnny was doing work for Dublin Gas and I knew him. It was 12.0 midnight and we had no money to pay him after he brought us back to the car.

'We asked him not to say anything to anybody... to Farrell or anybody, because we knew they would all jump to the wrong conclusions. Johnny had no tickets for the All-Ireland, and I was able to get him a pair. We were not back to Dublin till 1.30... 2.0 in the morning.'

At the start of 1989, with two All-Ireland titles at their backs and the tantalising prospect of a three in-a-row sitting prettily up in front of them, Galway headed off on the Allstars tour, from which the team returned without Tony Keady.

Brendan Lynskey was not on the tour, and had informed the county secretary and selector, Phelim Murphy that he could not take time off work. He'd decided to go on a holiday of his own at a later stage in the year.

When trouble brewed while Tony was still in New York, and his name was in lights for playing illegally in the championship in the city, Lynskey instinctively knew how it would all end.

'I spoke on the phone while Tony was out there and it was starting... and I warned him that they were going to try to make an example of him. We'd gone through four or five hard years of playing hurling at this stage, and all anyone was doing in the US was trying to make a few pounds.

'Nobody had any money back then, and all anyone wanted to do was to get on with their lives, get a roof over their heads... maybe meet someone... live their life. We had won two All-Ireland finals but, financially, nobody was any better off than they had been in '85.

'The year before that... sure I had been over there seven or eight times, and I had played with seven or eight different teams. I'd get a thousand dollars for the game... and I don't mind telling that. Everyone was doing it.

'I'd fly out on a Friday, and come home on the Monday.'

Brendan Lynskey is still angry all these years later, even more so after Tony's passing, that the GAA chose to make an example of his best friend. And he makes no apology for personally directing that anger at the late John Dowling, president of the association during that period.

'For the president of the most powerful organisation in the country... to go after one man... and look to make an example of Tony?

'Why would a man want to do that?

'Who would want that on their CV... how could John Dowling be proud of himself for going after Tony Keady and making an example of him in front of the whole country?

'I am still so angry about that... it was so wrong. What was John Dowling trying to prove to anyone?

'Tipperary voted for Tony, but we were beaten by two votes ... Leitrim and Roscommon. Can you believe people would think like that? Even still, I find it hard to understand the small-mindedness.

'Because... how people thought about Tony was copper-fastened for me when he died. The turn out... they all came!

'Babs and Nicky English, and all of the Tipp lads, and you can not believe how much we fought one another and wanted to beat one another all those years earlier. It was like we hated one another back then, but they all came. Lads from England... Donie O'Connell from the Middle East.'

Brendan Lynskey says they all knew how great Tony Keady was on the hurling field. Equally, he says they all remembered how gravely he had been wronged at the highest point of his career.

•••◆•••

THE BOTTOM LINE was that Keady and Lynskey were putting more time into their Galway hurling careers than anyone else in Cyril Farrell's camp. The hours and days and weeks through 1985 and '86 were mountainous.

But in 1987, with two All-Ireland final defeats still rattling around annoyingly in everyone's heads, they had to start from scratch all over again. 'No one knew the training we were doing,' Tony would later recall as he explained the regime himself and Lynskey had working for them. 'Myself and that man used to run on the road... five or six miles, and we used to train every single night of the week.

'You'd always do a bit of training on your own and no one would know about it, but by Jesus, we pushed one another to the limit when we trained together above in Dublin. I was working in the bank and used to do a bit of boxing with the Finglas boxing club.

'The first night I went training we went for a run on the road and I thought that would be grand, but when we got back to the club I discovered that the run was only the warm-up.

'In the gym afterwards... now that was training boy.'

In the opening months of the new season, Tony had different men either side of him in the half-back line and by the time Galway lifted the National league title he was flanked by Ollie and Tony Kilkenny.

Pete Finnerty and Gerry McInerney were in the United States and would not splash down – like two astronauts coming back down to earth – for a few weeks after that. Though everyone in the Galway dressing-room knew that the pair would be in peak condition when they did return home. Finnerty and McInerney were no fools – they knew the work that was being done 3,000 miles away from them.

From the vantage point of the Galway dressing-room, the summer looked promising. There was a league title in the bag, and on their way to that victory over Clare in Thurles, they had seen off Offaly and condemned their closest of neighbours to a visit to Division Two. Offaly looked out of luck, and further south there was dispiriting news for Cork when the immaculate Jimmy Barry Murphy called it a day.

Barry-Murphy had worn the red shirt since he was 19 years-old, and he had played football for the county until 1980. He retired with six All-Ireland medals in his pocket. A fair haul for anyone, but to a bunch of Galway hurlers, most of whom were working themselves to a standstill to win just one, such a bag of medals looked simply unbelievable.

Yes, the new league champions had every reason to be confident as they looked all around them. However, what they did not know was that their toughest opponents of all, and the team that would stand tallest with Galway in defining the end of the decade, were ready to make a spectacular appearance.

In the summer of 1987 Tipperary would run out onto Croke Park on a championship Sunday for the first time in 16 years.

They would share that Sunday with Galway.

••• ◆ •••

GALWAY HAD TRAMPLED all over Waterford in the league semi-final, winning by 5-16 to 1-12, a 16-point humiliation that formally commenced in the ninth minute of the game when Anthony Cunningham raced onto the end of a magical piece of play by Lynskey and Joe Cooney and planted the ball easily enough in the net. Cunningham would finish the game with a mighty tally of 3-3.

The prospect of some reward – *any* reward – after losing two All-Ireland finals was tantalising. No league title looked as valuable as the league title of 1987. Talking to Tom O'Riordan of the *Irish Independent* the week before the game, Tony spoke of Finnerty's absence and the almighty need to win something.

Anything.

'I have a particularly good understanding with Pete,' he mused. 'We played together since the under-16 team with Galway and we grew to know one another's styles over the years. He is a loss to Galway, but we are fortunate to have a very strong panel.

'The competition for places on the Galway team over the last year has kept us all on our toes and this is a very healthy situation. I believe you have

Tony and Margaret (photographed in their early days, below) were always happiest together.

Tony with Shannon on one of the family's visits to Knock and (below) with his daughter on the days of her Holy Communion and Confirmation.

Tony with his boys, Anthony, Harry and Jake during his Legends Tour of Croke Park in the summer of 2017 and (below) as a father he took such pride in being with his 'three men.'

Tony with Anthony on the day of his Confirmation (main), and with Harry at Croke Park and ready for some golfing with Jake.

One happy family together at a family wedding.

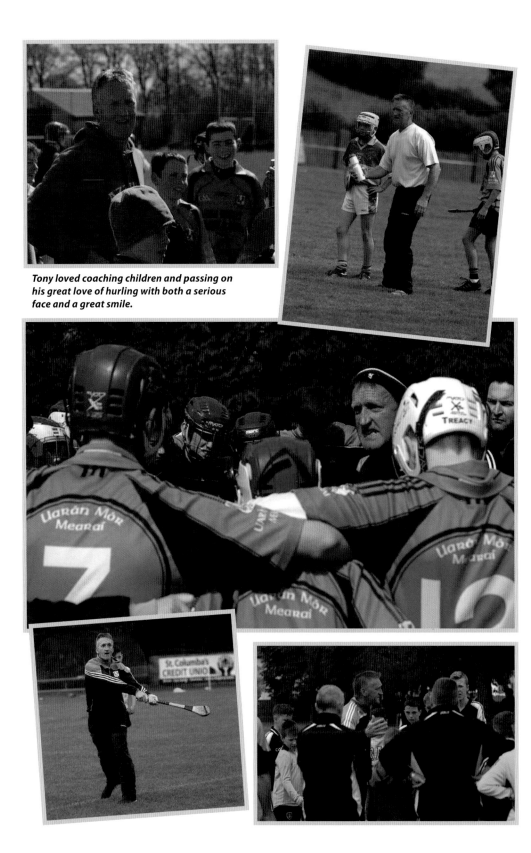

Tony loved coaching children and passing on his great love of hurling with both a serious face and a great smile.

Long after their playing days were over, Tony still had a great relationship with his two half-backs heroes from the 80s, Pete Finnerty and Gerry McInerney.

Galway, 1987 All-Ireland Champions.

Galway, 1988 All-Ireland Champions.

The King of centre-backs surveys the field in 1987 (main) and in 1988 getting to grips with Donie O'Connell of Tipperary in the All-Ireland final.

Tony crosses the field after Galway's loss to Tipperary in the 1989 All-Ireland semi-final which he missed due to suspension (top) and in action against Cork's Kevin Hennessy in the 1990 All-Ireland final.

The GAA community says a sad farewell to Tony in Croke Park during the 2017 All-Ireland final.

Joe Canning, the hero of Galway's 2017 All-Ireland win over Waterford, embraces Shannon on the field after the game (main) and manager Micheal Donoghue with Shannon and Joe.

One the day of the 2017 All-Ireland final supporters paid tribute to Tony in so many ways, including honouring the No.6 shirt he wore so proudly in the colours of Galway and his beloved Killimordaly.

Shannon and her brothers join Galway's Allstar winners at the 2017 banquet (top) and Shannon with Joe Canning who, like Tony in 1988, was voted the greatest hurler in the country in 2017.

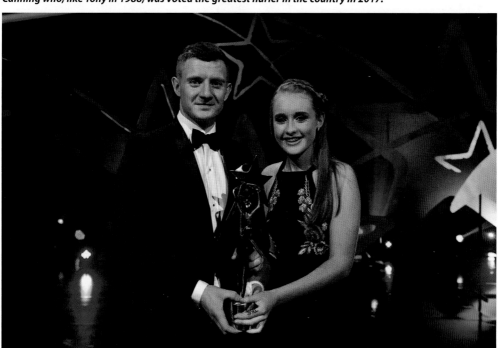

Tony and Margaret at the Opel GPA Gala Awards banquet in 2010.

yet to see the best of this team.'

However, Tony also took time out to remember his own time spent in the US, living in Boston, and travelling down to New York to play there as well, as he spoke to the *Independent* journalist. 'I actually took all my gear with me, but I seldom got a chance to use it,' he confessed. 'I missed hurling at home.

'And now we've got a chance to win something. I would dearly love to win this final. There is no point in thinking about the All-Ireland at this stage. We would not benefit from another loss, but I believe we are ready to beat Clare.

'There is a real determination to put it right this time, and our forwards are good enough to give us the edge. It's important we get it right.'

Clare were much tougher in the final than anyone imagined.

But Galway got it right, and captured their fourth league final success in six appearances, and got their hands on silverware that stemmed a worrying sequence of failing in finals, even if they just edged it 3-12 to 3-10.

There was a stubbornness and a fierce desire about Galway's play throughout a rollercoaster of a second-half, with each team landing hefty blows on the other's chin. In fact, Clare might have had the last and decisive score of the game, but Ger McInerney fumbled a long ball in from Michael Guilfoyle when he was straight in front of the posts and there was only 60 seconds left on the clock.

'The ball dribbled harmlessly through to Peter Murphy at the town end of the field and as the goalkeeper's long clearance soared away to safe regions in the mind's eye the accumulated gratitude of every Galway person present trailed like a banner behind it,' wrote Peadar O'Brien in *The Irish Press.*

Galway's stars on the day were Joe Cooney, who finished his afternoon's work with 2-6, Tony Keady and Tony Kilkenny, and Cunningham. Both of Cooney's goals came in the first-half and were against the run of play, as Cyril Farrell watched his men struggle to shake off their nerves.

They were lucky to lead 2-4 to 0-7 at the interval.

In the second-half, Clare rocked Galway further with two goals in two minutes to retake the lead, 2-7 to 2-6. Cunningham palmed home a goal from a Lynskey cross, but Clare were not to be shaken off and Syl Dolan scored their third goal to reduce Galway's advantage to a point.

But Galway made it home in the end.

Jim Carney: Admittedly Galway honestly expressed the view that the National league was not their priority at this point in the season but it was still extremely worrying that with the exception of the steady, secure Tony Keady none of the Galway rearguard played with the confidence or the conviction that marked the hurling of men further afield.

(Tuam Herald, May 6, 1987)

GALWAY WERE DUE to meet the Munster champions on August 9.

Farrell had given his two 'missing' defenders, Finnerty and McInerney, a deadline to fly out of New York and be back home a full month before the All-Ireland semi-final. They had to be home by July 1.

Meanwhile, as he put the final touches to his mind's tactical plans, Farrell had to have a word with one of the elders on the team. Farrell felt that the team needed more tricks up its sleeve in the biggest matches.

Two All-Ireland final defeats had told him that.

Galway needed surprises. And Farrell knew that Noel Lane was not going to be delighted at the idea of forfeiting his starting place on the team and being labelled a 'super-sub' instead.

It was a big conversation, and the courage of both men resulted in Galway having a big gun ready to aim at opposing defences in August and September.

In the meantime, Galway spent July watching more than anything else, and the Munster championship resulted in quite a feast for everyone outside the wire. All-Ireland champs, Cork had only managed to draw with Tipperary in the Munster final in Thurles on July 12. It was 1-18 each at the finish, and everyone struggled to catch their breath after an epic.

Seven days later, the pair went at it again, but this time in the strange surroundings of Fitzgerald Stadium in Killarney. And Tipp ended a 16-year wait by lifting the Munster title, winning 4-22 to 1-22, but only after extra-time.

Tipperary were the team everyone was now talking about.

Cork and themselves had been level, 1-17 each at full-time in the replay, but then the men in blue and gold, younger, fiercely hungry, surged for the finish line in added time. However, 89 minutes of play had to pass before manager, Babs Keating saw his team take the lead for the first time – when

Donie O'Connell put them in front, 1-22 to 1-21. It was the fourth minute of the second-half of extra-time. Then Cork caved completely, and three Tipp goals followed in the last nine minutes of the afternoon's play. Michael Doyle, who came on as a substitute, the son of the legendary John Doyle, scored two of them. O'Connell grabbed the third.

Tears flowed.

The Tipperary captain, Richard Stakelum spoke of the end of a famine.

Two years earlier, only 8,200 people had turned up in Croke Park to see Galway meet Cork in the All-Ireland semi-final. In August, 1987, over 50,000 would make their way to the ground.

Tipperary were the darling team of the summer.

As Miko Donoghue slowly crept the Galway team coach closer and closer to Croke Park the afternoon of the All-Ireland semi-final it was clear to everyone in the vehicle that the whole of Tipp seemed to be on the march on the footpaths surrounding the ground. When they arrived into their dressing-room, Tony Keady and his teammates found two large bundles of match programmes on the table in the middle of the room.

The front cover was coloured blue and gold, and the only man on the cover was Tipp's big hearted defender, Bobby Ryan.

There was no Galway player with him.

Inside the same programme there was a lengthy article on Babs, who had just led his county out of Munster and who had personally scored 2-12 for Tipperary when they had defeated Galway the last time the two teams had met in an All-Ireland semi-final, back in 1971, in Birr.

IT WAS VITAL to stem Tipperary's momentum.

Farrell knew that, and by the time the ball was thrown in to get a white-hot All-Ireland semi-final underway, every single Galway hurler understood what needed to be done, and preferably in the first few minutes of the game.

The pace never relented.

'At the end, Galway pulled away with a goal and a point in the dying minutes,' wrote Sean Kilfeather in *The Irish Times*, *'... to leave Tipperary as exhausted as the rest of us.'*

Although he had been named on the half-forward line, Farrell had promised his men that Nicky English would lead the Tipp attack, which he did, scoring the first point of the game after 15 seconds. If Tipp were the darling team of the summer of '87, then English was the darling player.

English was electrifying on the ball.

And Tipp sparked any time the ball went near him, but Farrell's men did what was asked of them and they led by five points after only eight minutes. The lead was increased to seven (1-10 to 0-6) after 26 minutes, but a goal from Pat Fox from the penalty spot brought Tipp closer by half-time, 1-13 to 1-9. After English's early point, John Commins' puck out had landed about 30 yards from the opposing goal and Lynskey found Martin Naughton with a fine pass and the winger drove the ball past Ken Hogan.

Tipp started the second-half even faster than they had the first – after 14 seconds O'Connell pointed, then Aidan Ryan added another, and next Paul Delaney landed a '65' to leave it at 1-13 to 1-12. Galway led by just one point.

Galway had bad wides from Michael McGrath and Steve Mahon, and Tipp dug even further. A Galway attack was broken up and the ball was swept down the field where Fox was waiting and he left McInerney in his wake as he raced 30 yards before driving the ball to the net. Tipp led 2-14 to 1-16.

English, who had moved out to the right wing, added a beautiful point, but vitally Cooney pointed a free and then Mahon levelled the game. And when Lynskey reacted brilliantly to a dropping free from Conor Hayes and set up Eanna Ryan with a well judged pass, Tipp suffered a goal from which they struggled to recover. Lane came into the game and nailed down the victory with a goal from close range.

It wasn't Tony Keady's greatest game. Donie O'Connell had only scored two points on him, but Tony knew he could do so much better.

He knew he would have to do better if Galway were to finally land the All-Ireland – the 100th All-Ireland hurling final in the rich history of the game.

'If we lost a third final in-a-row,' Tony estimated years later, '... definitely, it would have been curtains for me. I'd have been gone... absolutely.

'But, when we won, I remember thinking... *Jesus, we're still young enough... we could win this thing again!'*

Kilkenny awaited in the All-Ireland final.

And Farrell would warn his men, over and over, that Kilkenny always expected to win All-Ireland finals. He announced in the dressing-room that Galway's will to win would have to one hundred times greater than their opponents. He reminded them how often Kilkenny had beaten them, and how savage some of those defeats had been.

Farrell was thinking of the All-Ireland final defeats to Kilkenny in 1975 and '79, and all of the semi-finals that formed a large pile of disappointment – the teams had met 20 times in semi-finals and, before 1986, Galway had only managed to get by Kilkenny in 1953 and, before that, they had to journey back to the 1920s for a Galway victory party over Kilkenny.

Kilkenny knew that Galway were desperate. Their manager Pat Henderson counted on that, amongst other things, as a distinct advantage to the Cats.

Cyril Farrell: We'd have to beat them 10 times on the trot … just to get the balance right.

(September 2, 1987)

Pat Henderson: Desire for revenge is a bad thing... when you direct it at another team.

(September 2, 1987)

TONY KEADY OPENED the scoring in the 1987 All-Ireland final by sending a '65' soaring over the bar.

Soon, there were battles of all sizes and shapes being waged all over the field. The 100th All-Ireland hurling final would not be the prettiest. It was torrid, and it was tougher than tough. Farrell had wished for a dry sod, but the first Sunday in September was a complete washout.

Kilkenny found it harder to hit the ground, and they failed to score from play in the opening 35 minutes. Their four points were all converted by Ger Fennelly from placed balls, but Galway had only Tony's '65', two frees from Joe Cooney, and another couple from play to give them a 0-5 to 0-4 advantage. At the end of that half, the Cats had nine wides totted up. Galway, over the full 70 minutes, would only err with six strikes at goal.

In a game of numbers, Limerick referee Terence Murray would have Kilkenny's Ger Henderson, Richie Power, Ger Fennelly and Liam Walsh in his little black book, while Lynskey, Naughton and Hayes would also have to formally give their names to the same official.

FOR THE FIRST and only time in All-Ireland final history, Cyril Farrell had allowed a reporter into the team dressing-room, and into the dugout, for the whole day.

Martin Breheny, a Galway man, who had learned his trade in the *Tuam Herald* but was now working for *The Sunday Press*, was also one of Farrell's best friends. Farrell had actually allowed Breheny to join the team for three solid days.

And in the pages of the *Press*, Breheny told the inside story of what it was like in the Galway dressing-room at half-time in the 1987 All-Ireland final.

'Cyril Farrell squatted in front of his players, looking totally relaxed. Nobody was saying too much as mind and body unwound after 35 minutes of torrid action. Some fidgeted with boot laces, some visited the toilet, Martin Naughton was having his hand attended to, while others just sat there motionless, staring ahead.

'A steward dropped in, politely pointing to his watch. It was time to reappear for that dramatic period which would have such influence on Galway's hurling destiny.

'Farrell stood up. Outside, the Galway fans would be expecting him to deliver a spirited oration, pleading to the players' emotions and reminding them of previous failures in an effort to lift them for the second-half.

'He chose a completely different line.

' "Take a look at that scoreboard on the way out lads. It says five-four in our favour... just imagine that. We are a point ahead without playing well.

"Not bad, that. Now lads, we are going to be better in this half... and you know why? Because we are going to use our heads... we are going to hold together and we are going to take our men on.

"We are also going to open up the play and when you have that ball in your hand don't be afraid to take them on. You are better than them... so do things with confidence. And for God's sake, don't get involved in arguments either... with them or the referee.

"Relax.

"Lads we are ahead… and we are going to stay there."

'Captain Conor Hayes threw out a specific challenge.

"We are 35 minutes away from an All-Ireland title. And are we going to let it be taken away from us? We remember the dejection of the past few years.

"Are we going to make do with that again, or are we going up those steps for the cup? I have no doubts in my mind what we are going to do.

"Let's go out and do it then."

'Hayes concluded, thudding his hurley off the table as the team rose to its feet, determination flashing in every eye.

'Farrell took over again, just for a few seconds. He didn't want them to be depending solely on the dressing-room motivation.

"Remember lads… use your heads and you'll win.

"No question about it, but you have got to stay calm… and work together. That's going to win us this All-Ireland." '

IT WAS A day when a goal would definitely be precious, and of considerably greater value than just three points. Kilkenny were finding it hard to plunder any kind of score.

They would not get their goal.

Galway would nail one, and win the game 1-12 to 0-9 – with only three of those Kilkenny points coming from play. Only one of Kilkenny's starting forwards would manage to score from play.

'The excellence of the Galway defence is reflected in the fact that only three of Kilkenny's nine points came from play,' wrote Paddy Downey in *The Irish Times*. *'Only one of the original forward line up, Harry Ryan put his name on one of those and it was a superb effort from the right at the Canal End early in the second-half. Ger Fennelly, who finished with seven in all, scored the first from play half a minute after the restart and substitute Tommy Lennon struck the third nine minutes before full-time. Lennon's point was Kilkenny's only score in the last 26 minutes of the game.'*

The Galway defence was suffocating.

In *The Irish Independent* Vincent Hogan also spoke of heroic defending on a scale seldom witnessed in the grand old stadium.

'They will tell you around Mullagh and Kinvara that Peter Finnerty and Gerry McInerney are "mighty men." And who could doubt them when you see the latter smashing a hurley by merely testing its spring for a line-ball? For once Finnerty was a supporting role. McInerney hurled like a man who had been grievously insulted just before the throw-in. Nothing was ever going to stop him accompanying that cup across the Shannon tonight.'

The half-back line set up the winning of the game, but the winning stroke, the final nail in Kilkenny's coffin, was left to an older, wiser man up front.

Noel Lane was introduced early enough.

He came bounding onto the field in the 40th minute, and in the 63rd minute he pounced. Galway led by two points, 0-11 to 0-9. Kilkenny had a line ball under the Cusack Stand and close to the Canal End. Ger Fennelly struck it. Steve Mahon got his stick to the ball, and he batted it down and then doubled on it. The ball went to Eanna Ryan. He slipped by Sean Fennelly and took off.

Ryan carried the ball for 40 yards before passing it off to Cooney, who wove his way through a handful of defenders, before finding Lane.

Lane's shot was light, and the ball was deflected into the net from Kevin Fennelly's hurley. The ball squirmed over the line.

Tony belted over the last score of the game.

Gerry McInerney was voted the Man of the Match. Every Galway defender was in the running for the accolade, but McInerney was imperious.

Bernie O'Connor: We now have the Railway Cup, the National league and the Liam MacCarthy Cup and anyone who likes can come looking for them.
(September 7, 1987)

Cyril Farrell: Beating Kilkenny in a final leaves no room for any doubt.
(September 7, 1987)

Christy Heffernan: McInerney broke us. He broke our hearts. Their defence never gave us an inch to move. When you thought you were past your man there were two others running at you.
(September 7, 1987)

Noel Lane: The game was so close that I felt one goal could swing it. The thought was uppermost in my mind when I came on as a substitute. I got one chance and I missed it, and then I was thinking would I get another? Then the ball broke in front of me and I swung at it. The keeper had it covered and, in fact, he saved it but the ball rolled over the line. I think the Gods willed it in. But I think a team needs luck to win an All-Ireland.

(September 7, 1987)

Steve Mahon: In a way it's nearly sweeter than 1980 having lost two in-a-row. It was very physical in very humid conditions although the ground was fairly good. We missed a few chances but still we never let them into the game.

(September 7, 1987)

•••◆•••

AFTER GALWAY HAD defeated Kilkenny in a game that was sullen, sombre and then outrageously joyous when it was finally all over, Tony Keady decided on the Monday afternoon to drive his own car back to Galway. He did so behind the Galway team coach, in which the Liam MacCarthy Cup was perched in pride of place in the front window.

He knew that once the celebrations had ended that he would need to hightail it back to Dublin quickly enough.

So he kept the nose of his car tight to the rear of the bus. Except nobody knew that Tony was behind the wheel of his own car and, entering Ballinasloe, the cavalcade came to a standstill and Galway supporters began climbing onto the bonnet of the yellow Opel Kadett in order to get a proper look at some of their heroes.

Tony watched it all from the front seat of his car, and laughed.

When Galway completed the double, by defeating Tipperary once again in the 1988 All-Ireland final, Tony again had his homecoming diverted from the rest of the team. He was standing on a trailer in Loughrea, after being coaxed out of the team bus on this occasion, in order to say a few words.

'The tail of my shirt was sticking out and there was a load of my clubmates from Killimordaly at the back of the lorry,' he would remember. 'One of them… Noel Earls… a great friend of mine… jumped up and caught the back of the shirt.

'And didn't I fall off the back of the lorry… straight into their arms. They brought me to Mike Carey's pub and I think I was in it for three days!'

LEGEND

CHAPTER 4

1988

THE GALWAY HALF-BACK line was indeed a phenomenon.

In double quick time, it had become the most exhilarating line in the game of hurling. Finnerty, Keady and McInerney were compulsive viewing.

They were box office.

It was a line that was swashbuckling, and fearless, and one that did not at all conform to any set of old rules. But McInerney, initially, was reluctant to throw himself into the Galway set-up. And, even all of these years later, he finds it hard to fully explain why that was the case.

'We did not know too much about one another,' he admits.

'We never hung around. Tony was in Dublin... himself and Brendan Lynskey, and I hadn't played underage with him and at the start of Farrell's second time in charge I wasn't ready to get involved.'

Gerry McInerney liked the United States, but he was not one to hang around GAA clubs on the east coast to begin with. He played minor for Galway in 1983, and after that he headed over. He went to Arkansas, to Little Rock, a place that for 16 years future US President Bill Clinton called his home. Clinton was Arkansas Governor through most of the 80s.

McInerney was working in the leather business out there, and hurling was the least of his worries. In 1985, when he was working in New York, he still had to think long and hard about his life before deciding to commit his summers to Farrell and the Galway dressing-room.

He remembers a life without hurling fondly. 'The first year I was out there was great... a different life... living in Little Rock, and then I travelled down to Panama Beach in Florida. It was a long way from Galway.' And that was just fine for Gerry McInerney at that time.

It was a life that interested Pete Finnerty, and he joined McInerney. It was also a life that Tony Keady could not fully put out of his mind.

New York would call him too.

And New York would end up tripping Tony up, and causing a whole heap of trouble for him and the Galway team hell bent on winning a hat-trick of All-Ireland titles in 1989.

'Myself and Tony did not soldier together off the field, or anything like that,' McInerney says. But when the time came for the two of them, and also Finnerty, to build the strongest defensive wall in hurling they did so as though they had all been born to that exact task.

'Farrell called to our house at home with Phelim Murphy, when they were taking over and they wanted me in,' McInerney remembers. 'I didn't show too much interest at the start. We were playing Offaly in a challenge game at one stage... and I didn't show up.

'I was doing hay or something, I can't remember.

'It was not in my head to join the squad seriously at that stage. I needed more time... I was light-hearted about it. But then, finally, I made a decision that I wanted to do it and give it a real go.

'I came on board in 1986.

'We had a strong line from the start. We knew it... it just clicked with the three of us. It always felt right when the three of us were on the field together.

'We had great craic.

'We loved to get wired into the opposition.

'We knew we could do our own thing out there, and we never had to worry about one another. Even in training we had a fierce bond, and we'd look to never let the ball pass.'

McInerney had always played legally with clubs in New York, with the

Galway club to begin with, before changing to Laois, which was also full of Galway men who just happened to wear blue and white instead of maroon.

In '85 he won the New York championship, and was joined by other men from Farrell's dressing-room. 'Sean Treacy and Joe Cooney came out and we won the championship out there. We were all official and had all the paperwork right.

'Then Tony came out... and Tony wanted to play after the Allstars tour had finished. He ended up staying and playing. The Galway set up had not pulled together and we were playing for the Laois club. I didn't think it was a giant risk... there were a lot of lads playing illegally out there all of the time.

'You'd see them all of the time.

'It was a pity... what happened to Tony broke up everything really, and we never got back right again as a team after that.

'What they did to Tony really was the beginning of the end for the whole team.'

•••◆•••

BY THE END of 1987, Galway had played 13 competitive games. They had won ten of them, drawn three. In October the Railway Cup was lifted again when they beat Leinster, 2-14 to 1-4, and when the league resumed they beat Kilkenny by two points in Nowlan Park, drew with Tipperary, defeated Limerick by three points, completely ripped Clare apart, and drew with Cork. Galway were still striding out at the start of 1988, though the pack was not all that far behind.

Finally, in February, in Fraher Field in Dungarvan, for the first time in 15 months – since losing to Westmeath in the league in the autumn of 1986 – Farrell saw his men go down. In a seven-goal thriller, Waterford won 4-10 to 3-10. There followed a draw in Wexford Park. After that, Galway met Offaly in the league quarter-final in Croke Park.

Again, Galway went down.

They lost their league crown, and this second defeat sent a message out to every other team that Galway's All-Ireland crown might also be sitting perilously.

Admittedly, it was a Galway team that had the appearance of a jumbled selection – PJ Molloy was in for defender Ollie Kilkenny, Joe Cooney was out at midfield, Pearse Piggott was back in the left corner, and Tom Monaghan was in the half-back line. And it was still a game they should have won.

Offaly led 2-9 to 1-8 midway through the first-half, but Galway put in a big finish, and Molloy had them level (1-13 to 2-10) after he took his point from a penalty after Brendan Lynskey had been pulled down with the goal at his mercy. Lynskey then went for a goal when a point was for the taking, and he soon regretted that decision when Offaly broke out of defence and the ball was squeezed through to Mark Corrigan who swung it over for the winner.

•••◆•••

CYRIL FARRELL KNEW that his team needed to take a deep breath, lift themselves, and go again.

He also needed to be harder on them, if they were to even think of gloriously retaining the Liam MacCarthy Cup. On the day that Gerry McInerney was married, he ordered his players to leave the reception in Hayden's Hotel in Ballinasloe just after the meal. There was a training session to be undertaken.

Farrell wanted his players sharp, physically and mentally before they would appear in the All-Ireland semi-final on August 8 (when they would get the opportunity of revenging their league defeat by Offaly) and keeping them all on their toes for four long months was never going to be the easiest thing.

The players were back training with their clubs on Tuesdays and Thursdays. Farrell had them in on Mondays and Wednesdays, and if there was a club game on a Sunday afternoon, well, then Farrell also looked to squeeze in a challenge game that same weekend.

By the end of June, the players were all Farrell's four nights every week, and also all weekend, every weekend.

There was no reason for Galway to be headlining the national newspapers, but drama was already into the nasty habit of following the Galway team around like a stray dog. Pete Finnerty had taken a 12-month career break from the Garda Siochana in April of 1987 and when he played against the Allstars in the spring tour of 1988, he decided to stay put in New York. Steve

Mahon was also off the team in the spring due to a cartilage operation and then, in July, with an All-Ireland quarter-final against London on the horizon, Brendan Lynskey got himself into a whole heap of trouble.

He was sent off in a seven-a-side tournament in Dublin, playing for the Galway Association against a Tipperary selection in a competition organised by the Offaly Association. Quite complicated. Worse still, the competition was unauthorised, it turned out.

Lynskey was hit with a three months suspension.

Late night phone calls ensued, and trips to Croke Park by Farrell and his lieutenants, before the suspension was lifted with immediate effect by a meeting of the GAA's Central Council.

•••◆•••

WEXFORD, AFTER BEATING Kilkenny had been favourites for the Leinster title, but Offaly broke their hearts with the decisive score of the afternoon after George O'Connor cleared the ball hastily from his own square, only to find Michael Duignan. He centred, Wexford goalkeeper Paul Nolan hesitated, and then fell to his knees to smother the dropping shot. Joe Dooley was in like a light for his goal. Offaly won 3-12 to 1-14, and deep in Munster Tipperary held onto their provincial crown, and quite majestically at that, taking Cork by 2-19 to 1-13 in the final.

In the All-Ireland semi-final Galway were looking to redress the 3-1 advantage that Offaly held over them in All-Ireland semi-finals and finals over the previous eight years. They would do so clinically, and without playing to their very best, finishing up 3-18 to 3-11 and securing a first meeting with Tipp in an All-Ireland final since way back in 1958.

'Long term forecasts remain on course,' wrote Paddy Downey in The Irish Times. 'Galway and Tipperary are through to the All-Ireland hurling final on September 4th – the first clash of these counties for the Liam MacCarthy Cup since 1958. After an unsettled opening 30 minutes Galway frequently showed the class of champions when disposing of Offaly's disappointing challenge in the second semi-final at Croke Park yesterday.

'The promise of a great contest was not fulfilled for the 37,954 spectators but

Galway supporters were more than pleased with the team's performance once the forwards found their rhythm and the scores began to flow.

'Offaly kept closely in touch for nearly half an hour, during which times the scores were level four times, yet the game never flowed during that period, as if each team were sizing up the other and fearful of making mistakes.'

Galway grabbed their three goals in the first half and led 3-8 to 1-7 at the change. Noel Lane, in from the start, scored one of the goals, and four points as well. Martin Naughton and Eanna Ryan snatched the other two.

'Noel Lane had made a triumphant return to the team,' continued Downey. *'The born-again full-forward played a great game against no less an opponent than Offaly captain, Aidan Fogarty. He scored 1-4 and strongly challenged Naughton for the title of Man of the Match. Naughton, who scored 1-5, deserves that accolade however for his brilliant performance all through the game.'*

••• ◆ •••

TONY KEADY WATCHED, and admired, the way in which Cyril Farrell always sought to have the team finely tuned.

And, like the others who had heard Farrell talk of quitting in 1987, whether Galway won or lost the final, he secretly feared the schoolteacher from Woodford turning his back on them all. In '88 Tony knew that retirement was still on the manager's mind.

'He had his own way to keep things together,' Tony observed. 'He had a great way with him He was always out and about, and you'd meet him everywhere.

'In fairness, he was a manager who would always give you a bit of leeway because he'd know that you worked hard and he'd always get the best out of you.

'You'd go into a restaurant when you'd be having a meal and Farrell would go around to every single player in the restaurant. You'd be eating your dinner, and he'd put his hand in and he'd take a chip off your plate and have a few words.

'Before he sat down to eat himself he had enough ate. He was that kind of fella who'd have a word with everyone and he was good to get on with, and he'd have a bit of a laugh at training.

'Once lads are having a bit of a laugh they'd hardly know they are working hard at the same time and he knew that.

'He had a special team,' stated Tony fondly, '… but he was a special man.

'He knew how to handle us.

'He wasn't a school principal for nothing.'

Farrell, however, was still insisting and forewarning his team and their supporters that he was ready to go at the end of the summer.

Win or lose to Tipp.

Farrell felt he needed to find new ways and means of keeping his team on edge – and he also knew that he could not keep concocting new angles to training sessions. Though in the summer of '88 he had taking a liking to 9.0 am starts to training sessions. He knew the lads hated the thought of them.

'I'd see their faces,' Farrell remembers, 'and I'd know that they did not fancy it, but I also knew by the look of them that they were not going to let me try to get the better of them in any way.'

The grumbling in the dressing-room before the 9.0 am starts left the team boss certain that it was going to be a decent workout. After that, they would have a late breakfast together, and the remainder of the day belonged to his players.

Farrell also liked to surprise the lads with the 9.0 am starts.

One Friday evening, in Athenry, after a training session that he felt was sluggish at best he walked into the dressing-room and shouted, 'RIGHT!'

'That was awful, lads!

'It's not good enough… and I want you all to be here at ten to nine in the morning! And I want everyone…

'Do you hear me… EVERYONE… YOU HEAR ME?

'EVERYONE ON TIME!

'Have you got that?'

Heads nodded all around him.

The following morning Farrell slept-in. The road from Woodford to Kenny Park in Athenry was only touched on the occasional spot.

It was 9.15 am when the manager arrived. The car park was full. But there was nobody doing anything out on the field. It then dawned on Farrell that he had taken all of the sliothars home with him the night before in the boot of his car.

The lads were waiting for him.

Hands were on hips. Others were chatting in smaller groups. One or two were enjoying some of the early morning sun, and when Farrell's head appeared at the top of the small hill looking down upon the field, the slow hand clapping started.

At any time of the day, early morning or evening, they were a tight, happy crew. They knew one another. They liked one another's company.

They understood one another.

And the players knew full well that Farrell was doing all he could to get them exactly right, and at the same time to butter up Tipperary, as the big day approached.

Cyril Farrell: When you pick any team, you are taking a gamble in every position. Even the greatest players can fall down on the day. We have picked a team to play to our pattern, and to win.

Tipperary are a good team, with steady backs, the best midfield in the game, and exciting forwards. Nicholas English is a class apart, the best forward in hurling.

But we won't worry about Tipperary.

We worry about ourselves.

(September 2, 1988)

Michael 'Babs' Keating: I wouldn't get carried away with a Galway team who beat an Offaly side having Pat Delaney and Eugene Coughlan at centre-forward and full-forward. That was not a particularly good Offaly side... yet in the final 25 minutes they had Galway rattled.

Okay, we weren't over-impressive in the match against Antrim but what a lot of people don't realise is that Antrim have a strong and physically powerful team who are no pushover for anyone. When our forwards had possession against Antrim they were continuously put under pressure by their markers. I don't think the same thing could be said of the Offaly backs... the Galway forwards were given yards and yards of free space. I would expect that to change slightly on Sunday.

(September 2, 1988)

Brendan Lynskey: If we were playing Kilkenny or Cork this year I don't think we'd win. But Tipperary are different. Have Tipperary a God-given right to be favourites? We needed an injection (this year) and that will give it to us. We're going out to prove that we are champions.

We are fed up listening about Tipperary... Tipperary... Tipperary. What have they achieved to make them favourites? Two Munster titles and a league success hardly match our achievements over the last three years. We needed a lift this season, and Tipperary have given it to us.

(September 3, 1988)

Nicky English: I don't honestly think I was too satisfied with my performance last year. Conor just seemed content to shepherd me out the field, away from the danger zone... maybe there were times when I should have set my sights on goal. Last year is gone... maybe we stormed up to Croke Park on a tide of emotion... yet there was very little between the sides at the end.

We mightn't be playing great hurling this year, yet we've won our matches by eight or nine points. I'm not too worried about the Antrim match and I'm not over-concerned about Galway either. We have our own game to get right... if we do that, I believe we'll be All-Ireland champions on Sunday evening.

(September 3, 1988)

THE ALL-IRELAND FINAL would mark the centenary of the first championship final, that of 1887, which was played in Birr on April 1, 1888. Tipperary that famous day were represented by Thurles Blues. Meelick represented Galway.

Tipp won 1-1 to 0-0.

On their way to the 1988 final Tipp had beaten Limerick 0-15 to 0-8, Cork 2-19 to 1-13, and Antrim 3-15 to 2-10. Galway had beaten London 4-30 to 2-8, and Offaly 3-18 to 3-11.

••• ◆ •••

IN THE 1988 All-Ireland final there were four points in it at half-time.

Galway led 0-10 to 0-6.

Galway had seven wides.

Tipp six.

Tony Keady was inspirational at the gateway to the Galway defence.

Equally, Noel Sheehy looked unbeatable on the other side of the field in a contest that showcased two of the greatest half-back lines in the game performing at their very best

It was a game of the finest of margins.

The following morning, in the *Irish Independent*, Donal Keenan wrote on behalf of a whole country that had been transfixed for over 70 minutes.

'The Munster champions came very close to victory. Two superb feats by Galway players foiled them in a hectic finish. The first of these was a magnificent save by goalkeeper John Commins when the champs were hanging onto a two point lead, and then a great goal by substitute Noel Lane as the game turned into injury time.

'All-Ireland finals have seldom come harder than this one. It did not produce the fluent, open hurling which wishful thinkers had been predicting but it was a fierce contest in which both defences dominated for long periods.

'Galway led all the way, were six points in front at one stage in the first-half and four to the good at the interval. But Tipp cut the champions lead to a single point three times in the second-half when playing into the Railway goal with the brisk wind behind them.

'The Galway defence was heroic, especially in that second-half when Tipperary scented victory and pursued it with everything they had. After all the doubts about his ability to contain English, Conor Hayes rose to the occasion splendidly and for good measure scored a first-half point from a 90 yard free.

'Ollie Kilkenny was as steady as a rock in the left corner and after a hesitant first-half Sylvie Linnane, whose anticipation was almost perfect, closed off the other side of the field when ends were changed.

'But what can one say about the champions' half-backs that would adequately convey the power of their performance – particularly the majestic hurling of Gerry McInerney and Tony Keady? Pete Finnerty, on the right, was not as prominent as either of his colleagues but he, too, came up trumps when the effort was needed.

'*McInerney struck a fine point from behind midfield in the 23rd minute and in the 27th minute of the second-half, having caught a high ball, sent over an inspirational score, also from long range to put Galway three points in front at a crucial stage of the proceedings.*

'*Keady, in the centre, who struck two points on the day (one from a '70') was the hero of the second-half – the rock on which Tipperary's hopes perished more than any other, with the arguable exception of Commins, whose save from Cormac Bonner prevented Tipperary from taking the lead by one point with two minutes of normal time remaining.*

'*Commins parried Bonner's shot from close range and, then, with lightning speed, turned the bouncing ball out for a '70' which Delaney sent wide. Galway were still in grave danger, however, but they soon struck the mortal blow.*

'*Substitute Tony Kilkenny sent a long ground shot through to Lane, who had moved into the centre from the left corner. The Tipperary full-back, Conor O'Donovan turned to chase the ball but it spurted away from him. The full-back was isolated, his cornermen were nowhere to be seen. Lane sprinted on and with a crisp ground stroke buried the ball behind Ken Hogan.*'

Cyril Farrell: That's it. I have made up my mind… I'm gone. It's time for someone else to take over.

They fought like hell. The backs and midfield did well but the forwards played like backs in the second-half. It was a great team effort. I told them at half-time if we kept hurling and got to the ball first, we would win. They are the best bunch of hurlers we have ever had. All this talk about us being there before, that it would make it easy… that was hogwash. It is never easy, no matter how many times you reach an All-Ireland final.

(September 5, 1988)

Michael 'Babs' Keating: Keady broke our hearts.

I am disappointed with a few players, but overall I am not disappointed. I said all week that I dreaded a windy day. This Tipp team needs to play for 70 minutes, but in view of the wind they were only able to play for 35 minutes.

I have told them to stick it out and if they are men they will be back to win an All-Ireland, and if they do not come back we will know that they haven't the guts. Look at Theo English. He played for five years for Tipp without winning anything. He was 28 when he won his first all-Ireland... and he went on to win five.

(September 5, 1988)

Tony Keady: There is no two ways about it, but that Cyril Farrell must wait on. He has done so much for this team... he just couldn't go now.

It went well for me in the first-half. I knew when Joe Cooney and Eanna Ryan came back that we would hold out. We closed them down, and I think we proved ourselves today. It would be nice to think about winning three in-a-row next year, but we'll enjoy this one first. There was too much made of Tipperary and we came here determined to play our own game.

Halfway through the first half I heard Babs telling Nicky English to move out a bit, away from the goals... out to the middle of the field.

Even if the ball is not coming in as often to a player like English, you don't go putting him out the field. By waiting inside one ball might break for him and if he's doing his job that's a goal. A forward like him has his job to do and he won't do it 60 or 70 yards from goal.

(September 5, 1988)

Nicky English: To win we needed to draw level or even go ahead of them in the second-half. We failed to do so and that was our downfall. It will take us days, weeks... months to get this disappointment out of our system, but hopefully in the end everything will come right for us.

(September 5, 1988)

Brendan Lynskey: I thought we were a bit relaxed going into the match. Maybe that is experience, but how do you judge that? I thought we needed an injection. Tipperary thought they had a God-given right to win this All-Ireland. John Doyle said you only play Galway in challenge matches. There is no need for a pep talk after that. I do not know if Tipperary will come good. It will be a great test for them next season.

(September 5, 1988)

•••◆•••

ON A TUESDAY morning, early in January of 1989, Cyril Farrell picked up his newspaper and read that Galway's 26 year-old centre-back, Tony Keady was emigrating to the United States.

Farrell knew that everyone reading the same paper, elsewhere all over the county, would probably be in a state of shock. The reigning All-Ireland champions, instead of bolstering themselves for an historic three in-a-row, appeared to have players with other things on their minds.

Finnerty and McInerney liked the east coast of the States. Now Keady was saying he was going, and not much further into 1989 there would be talk of Lynskey also heading out of the country, to either New York or London.

Farrell, however, was not panicked.

Tony had told his manager of his intentions. He said he would be heading off, and further informed Farrell that he was going the morning after the Allstars banquet in Dublin on February 4.

Farrell was prepared to wait and see what transpired. Words, often or not, ended up only as words. He himself had insisted he was quitting as manager in 1987 and again in '88, but in the opening weeks of '89 he was still the Galway hurling manager.

He'd wait to see what Tony would finally do.

He knew that Tony was desperately keen to spend some time living in New York, and at the same time, he knew how the man lived and breathed Galway hurling. Farrell found it hard to imagine Tony missing out on the 1989 All-Ireland hurling championship defence.

He did not see it happening.

And, how was he to know the decision on Tony Keady's participation in Galway's All-Ireland defence would actually be taken out of the hands of the pair of them.

CHAPTER 5

1989

ALL OF THE pressure seemed to be sitting down upon the roof of the Tipperary dressing-room. They had failed to get by Galway on several occasions, and their momentum coming out of Munster had stalled. In 1989, it was down to Michael 'Babs' Keating and his team to stand up even taller, and deliver.

Galway, in comparison, just had to keep the engine revving.

In fact, all Galway had to do was sit back, stay calm, and observe all around them – see who was going to try to take their All-Ireland crown. Except, it didn't turn out like that. The year of the historic assault on a three in-a-row would implode on the reigning champs.

But Keating had no idea that anything like that would happen, and when he sat down with Tom O'Riordan of *The Sunday Independent* at the beginning of the year it was the mercurial Babs who was certainly defensive – to the point of suggesting that retaining their league title might even be a mistake.

'At the end of the day, this team will be measured by what it achieves in the championship,' stated the Tipp manager.

'After our defeat in the All-Ireland final many people in the county seemed to express the view that perhaps we should not have put so much effort into winning the league.

'It is hard to expect players to training diligently from February, win two major finals (league and Munster) and then expect them to be at their prime again a few weeks later.'

With his selectors, and former teammates, Theo English and Donie Nealon, Keating was in agreement that the league should not be his team's priority, or even second on their list. He had allowed his players time to recuperate after the All-Ireland final defeat, and asked nothing of them from between September and February.

'We just left it to the players themselves,' he explained. 'It can be a long summer, as we learned last year. I do not want to turn around next September and say that I wished that we did it a little differently. We are gearing ourselves for June 11. That is the day we play Limerick (or Kerry) in Pairc Ui Chaoimh and hopefully we can take it from there.'

However, Tipperary would still manage to get to the league final, and there they would find themselves in Galway's company – and dicing with the prospect of losing to Farrell's men for a fourth time on the major stage.

•••◆•••

KEADY'S MOVE TO US WILL HINDER GALWAY

The headline in *The Irish Times* on the morning of January 12, 1989, sent a shiver down too many spines. The opening paragraph of the article written by the venerable GAA correspondent Paddy Downey was also prophetic.

'Galway's hopes of winning a third successive All-Ireland hurling title this year received a heavy and, quite possibly, a mortal blow within the last week. Their brilliant centre half-back, Tony Keady, one of the mainstays of the champions' powerful defence, has decided to emigrate to the United States and, unlike his half-back line colleagues, Peter Finnerty and Gerry McInerney, in recent years, may not be able to return and play with Galway in the All-Ireland championship.'

Downey further reported that 'strenuous' moves were being made to keep Keady at home, but that he was 'determined' to be in Boston within three weeks.

The morning after the Allstar awards for 1988 were handed out in Dublin's Burlington Hotel, when Keady was due to pick up his second accolade – and

Galway were due seven recipients – was still the date for departure.

February 4.

Downey also reminded his readers that Tony's 'other half', Brendan Lynskey, who had announced his retirement after the 1987 All-Ireland win but was persuaded to give it one more go, had still to make up his mind about what he would be doing in the year ahead.

'If Tony quits,' Downey quoted Lynskey, '… I wouldn't relish the thought of driving alone from Dublin to Galway for training and back the same night, several times every week.'

•••◆•••

HOWEVER, WHEN CYRIL Farrell named his team to meet Limerick in the Gaelic Grounds in the league on February 19, the names of both Tony Keady and Brendan Lynskey were still on the sheet of paper.

The word was that Tony had postponed his trip to the US for the time being. Galway already had four wins in the league at their backs. It was harder to jump ship than either Tony or Lynskey had imagined.

Galway would win 1-14 to 1-8, in a bit of a canter in truth, on a sod that was hardly playable after a deluge of rain. There was nothing stopping Farrell's men – and with Tipperary due in Ballinasloe on the first Sunday in March it was additionally hard for anyone to even think of absconding.

Not only were Galway determined to keep Tipp under their thumb, but they were extra determined not to let any one member of the Munster champions' squad relieve himself of that sinking feeling. And when Babs Keating made it known that he was bringing a skeleton team – one without Nicky English, and also minus Ken Hogan, Bobby Ryan, Declan Ryan, John Kennedy, Pat Fox and John Leahy – there was some uproar amongst Galway supporters.

Babs said he wanted to give all of the players in his squad a run out, and since Tipp were well on their way to a knockout place in the league it was a logical enough explanation. Except, Tipp were playing Galway!

And Babs and Co. were accused of ducking their fiercest opponents, and looking to live and play, and hopefully win, another day.

Downey seemed as incensed as many supporters. *'Michael Keating and his fellow selectors have the right, of course, to select any team they like,'* he announced in the *Times. 'They are the bosses in their own house. But that right doesn't relieve them of their responsibilities to their own and their rivals' supporters, and to the game of hurling itself.'*

'We put it up to them!' Babs declared after the game in Ballinasloe.

They had put it up alright, but Tipperary had once again gone down (0-12 to 1-7) in Duggan Park. It turned into quite a fierce contest – with Keady and Declan Carr of Tipperary both booked after a second long-winded flare-up in the first-half of the game – but Joe Cooney's return to peak form made the difference on the afternoon as he brilliantly struck seven points, six of them from frees.

The teams had been level, 0-4 each at the interval, each scoring three times in the opening seven minutes of the contest, before things settled. Then Tony struck over a '70' and Sean Nealon replied for the visitors.

With a good win at their backs, Galway ran up a lead of four points, 0-9 to 0-5, after 17 minutes of the second-half, but it was back down to a point when Nealon slotted home a penalty for Tipp. Galway just did enough. And while Tipperary appeared very pleased with themselves, and the efforts of many of their fringe players, they were back to square one a few weeks later – and once again facing the prospect of contending with Galway in the league final.

•••◆•••

GALWAY WERE FAR too good for Dublin the league semi-final.

Everyone was still on board, and Tony shot over three points (one '70' and two long range frees) in their 2-13 to 1-9 victory.

Tipperary reported a lengthy injury list for the final – no Nicky English, no John Kennedy, no Pat Fox. This time Babs was putting out the best team he could select, and seeking for a fifth time to get the better of Farrell. There were three defeats and one draw (in a league tie in Thurles) on Tipperary's report card against Galway.

However, Galway would win again, and take Tipp's league crown by 2-16 to 4-8. This time Tipperary gave it all they had, and nobody realised that more than Brendan Lynskey who took two fierce knocks in the first-half, and had to retire six minutes into the second-half after suffering a facial injury. Tipperary also put themselves into positions to actually win the game.

Joe Hayes missed a goal chance in the first-half when, with no Galway defender within touching distance and only goalkeeper John Commins to beat, he hit fresh air instead of the ball on the 20 yards line. In the second-half the Tipp captain, Pat McGrath missed two scoreable opportunities from frees.

Farrell had no reason to be all that pleased with his men, who were heading off to the United States four days after the game. Joe Cooney (1-7), Gerry Burke (1-2) and Eanna Ryan (0-3) reached a total of 2-12 between them which also said a lot about the lack of accuracy of others around them, but more worrying the half-back line – the steely spine of the team – was off-colour.

Finnerty, who had been married the previous week, was replaced in the second-half, and it took Tony longer than anyone expected to take control of the centre of the defence, and he had his hands full with first Hayes, and then Donie O'Connell. In the *Irish Independent*, Vincent Hogan only gave Tony 6 out of 10 in his player ratings.

Hogan, however, had his suspicions about all the contestants.

'Even when yesterday's battle was moving towards its highest pitch,' he wrote, *'the suspicion remained that we are witnessing a war of minds. August deliverance may never come for Tipperary's disciples, but the thoughts of an All-Ireland collision never quite left this argument.*

'Tipp were beaten, it seemed, more by conviction than by ring-craft. Technically, Cyril Farrell's rulers have little to spare over their chief pretenders to their crown. But you sense that they now believe the Gods to be their children. Galway have no peers in self-esteem.

'They won yesterday, essentially, because they believed. There is something calm, something reasoned, about their approach to crises. Keady will clear a monster; Lynskey will catch a stray one; Cooney will find a score. Put it up to Galway and they have perfected the art of slamming it back in your face.'

Hogan's absolute confidence in Galway and his use of the word 'crises' was interesting, pertinent, and wholly significant with what lay around the corner.

••• ◆ •••

'THAT PROOF MUST come from new York. We can't take disciplinary action against any player on the basis of newspaper rumours,' explained GAA PRO, Danny Lynch on the final Monday in May. He was speaking to newspaper reporters, and was not being shy about informing them that the association needed more than their word for it that Tony Keady had played illegally in New York eight days earlier (on May 21) for the Laois club against the Tipperary cub, without the triple sanctions of his club and county secretaries, and also the Director General of the GAA.

Two other members of the Galway hurling squad, Aidan Stanton and Michael Helebert, were also in the same hot water – and facing the possibility of what appeared an outlandish 12-month suspension.

The three of them had travelled to the east coast of the US with the team for the Bank of Ireland Allstar matches on May 7 and 15. But they had remained behind when the full travelling party got on the coach to the airport the day after the second of those games.

They had played for Laois, who had beaten Tipp in the New York championship by 4-14 to 3-6. They had also played, strangely enough, under the names of Bernard Keady, Enda Staunton and Tom Helebert.

The GAA PRO was at pains to point out that if there was any substance to the reports the matter would have to be dealt with initially by the New York GAA Board, as it had finally affiliated itself to the association after many years of living outside of Croke Park's direct rule.

'New York can deal with it only if an objection is lodged by the Tipperary club,' continued Lynch. 'If such an objection was upheld, we would then have to get all the facts of the case before taking any action here.'

He added that if there was no enquiry by the NY Board, or if an objection from the Tipperary club was not sustained, then the GAA authorities in Dublin would have no grounds for disciplinary action.

On the face of it, the trouble that Tony Keady and his teammates were facing seemed a long way off. There were lots of hoops for the whole saga to be thrown through before anyone faced a ruinous year-long suspension!

But rules were still rules.

And the relevant rule in the Official Guide of the association stated that players intending to play within the New York Board area had to have official authorisation form, in duplicate, from their club and county secretaries, and the Director General. The rule stated that such forms needed to be lodged in Croke Park at least two days before the stated game.

And, GAA's congress had only lately stuck on one more ruling to this same page of the Guide – stating that official authorisation to play in New York is not valid unless the player concerned has remained in the area for a period of not less than 28 days.

THE NEXT MORNING, the daily newspapers were also of the belief that a suspension was unlikely.

The Tipperary club had not lodged an objection.

Which made Rule 143 of the Official Guide in the GAA extremely relevant. It stated that an objection by one team against another for any alleged irregularity must be lodged with the secretary of the committee in charge of the fixture within seven days of the starting time of the game. Ten days had passed by since Tony had played for the Laois club.

Any objection coming from the Tipperary club would have to be ruled out of order once it appeared before the New York president, Terry Connaughton.

Tony was in the clear, surely?

The New York Board had only affiliated itself to the Central Council of the GAA 12 months before – before formally becoming part of the GAA family the NY Board was not obliged to conform to Official Guide rules. Now, it needed to tow the association's line. Surely?

It looked good for Tony, for sure.

'If an objection from the Tipperary club is ruled out of order tonight,' wrote Paddy Downey in *The Irish Times, '... on the technical grounds outlined, the New York Board have no other means through which to assimilate proof that Keady, Staunton and Helebert broke any rules at all.'*

TWO DAYS LATER, there was a twist.

The story – which would become titled 'The Keady Affair' – would continue to twist itself in lots of places.

The Tipperary club lodged their objection with the New York Board.

And the New York Board accepted it and ignored Rule 143. But the Board postponed the hearing of the case for a fortnight, as the Laois club representatives said that they were not prepared to answer the charges levelled against them.

Before they became affiliated to the GAA back home, New York had preferred to operate under one of their own local rules – which gave a team 10 days, and not seven, to think long and hard before thumping an objection down on the table.

The whole untidy business was now in danger of becoming something of a saga, and a confusing one at that, though in the *Times*, Downey still had his nose in the middle of things.

'Although the Official Guide rules regarding objections is clear cut, the New York Board may invoke another rule,' explained the journalist, *'which enables an overseas committee of the association to apply to the Central Council for permission to deviate from any of the general rules in special circumstances.'*

There were, it appeared, rules in the Official Guide that stopped everyone in their tracks, and there were other rules that could be navigated around.

'There is no indication so far that the New York Board will take that course, or, if they do, that the Central Council would agree that the circumstances of the case warranted deviation,' continued Downey.

'The Tipperary club's objection – dated May 27, but not in the hands of the Board until Wednesday night – is based on two points. 1, That Keady, Staunton and Helebert were not entitled to play for the Laois club because they had been in New York with a visiting team (Galway) and were not resident there for the prescribed period of time. 2, That they played under false names.

'If the Tipperary objection is upheld on June 15th, the Laois club will then have the right to appeal the case to the Games Administration Committee or Management Committee in Ireland.'

OUT OF THE blue it was alleged that Babs Keating was stirring things in the whole saga, an accusation that the Tipperary manager strenuously denied.

'I had no contact with the Tipperary club in New York and I'd be a terrible idiot to get involved or express any opinion on the affair,' Babs thundered.

'I've never made bad friends anywhere in hurling... and I don't intend to do so now. Tipperary's record with regard to objections is clean.

'We like to win our games on the field.

'Everyone in Tipperary wants us to beat Galway in the championship and, what's more, beat them with a team which includes Tony Keady.

'That's how the Tipperary selectors and the players feel too.'

MEANWHILE, IN NEW York there was agreement being reached not to go for any nuclear option with the saga. Word on the streets was that the three Galway lads would get a suspension, or in other words, a stinging slap across the backs of their legs in public, but nothing more than that.

The suspension would stop short of August 6, the date of Galway's All-Ireland semi-final meeting with the champions from Munster.

AND TONY AND the two lads did look free, for a little while.

In the middle of June, the New York Board by way of a majority decision suspended the three of them for two matches. The Board accepted the explanation of the Laois club that the three of them had used false names, but, in fact, had all played under their 'middle' names, namely Bernard Keady, Enda Staunton and Tom Helebert.

The Laois club was told they were forfeiting the game to the Tipperary club, and that seemed the end of the whole affair. Once the GAA bosses in Croke Park accepted the decision of the New York executive committee!

Once they nodded their heads to New York!

It looked good.

Danny Lynch (GAA PRO): Any further consideration of the case will be a matter for the Games Administration Committee. I cannot predict, nor would I want to pre-empt, what they may decide.

(June 17, 1989)

Terry Connaughton (New York Board president): I believe this is a significant step forward in our efforts to stop the traffic of players from Ireland. This is the first time that players from Ireland have been penalised and the match points stripped from the offending team and awarded to their opponents. That's a deterrent. I hope the GAC and the authorities in the GAA will be happy with what we have done. I think they should be, even though we haven't complied fully with Official Guide rules.

(June 17, 1989)

Phelim Murphy (Galway Hurling Board secretary): The case of the three players is different to those who travel to New York for weekends and play there. Keady, Staunton and Helebert were in New York officially with the Galway team and decided to stay on and find work. In that situation, I believe that the allegations made against them shouldn't be dealt with in the ordinary way.

(June 17, 1989)

•••◆•••

IT WAS PERHAPS not the best time in the world for Tony Keady to state his own case, but he did so that same week by taking a phone call from Martin Breheny in *The Sunday Press*.

'I WAS ASSURED I COULD PLAY'

The headline to the article on Sunday, June 18, afforded Tony the opportunity of pleading his innocence, and he did so with conviction. 'If I knew I was doing anything wrong,' he stressed, 'I would never have played in New York.'

He argued that he had been given every assurance by the Laois club officials that no harm would come to him playing for them. Neither had he any clue about all of the authorisation forms.

'The whole affair has shocked me,' he told Breheny. 'I decided at the very last minute not to return home with the Galway team on the Allstars trip. It was such a late decision, that all of my baggage, including my hurleys, were brought home with the rest of the Galway gear.

'I was going to go up to my brother in Boston when I was approached to play for the Laois club against Tipperary on the following Sunday. I took a spur of the moment decision to stay on. On the day of the game my brother arrived from Boston and asked me if everything was in order to allow me to play in New York.

'Seeing as I had been in New York for two weeks with the team and that everybody knew I was there, I assumed it was okay to play. However, I checked with the people involved with the Laois club and told them that under no circumstances would I do anything that might interfere with the Galway team. They told me that there was nothing to worry about and that I was cleared to play. I accepted that.

'Once I wasn't going home with the Galway lads, I decided to get myself a job and stay for some weeks. I assumed that I could play with a club in New York and the Laois officials kept repeating there was nothing to worry about.

'Does anybody seriously think that if I thought I was doing anything wrong I would have played?

'I want to be part of Galway's three in-a-row bid, so I would not have taken the chance if I thought I was ineligible to play. After all, it's not as if I wouldn't be recognised.

'I knew absolutely nothing about getting written clearances in duplicate, etc, etc... and I can tell you that most players out there don't either.

'The place is crawling with Irish hurlers and footballers... most of them 'weekenders'. Yet nothing happens... and I can tell you most of them have no clearances from home. So why would there be one rule for inter-county players and another for club players? I hope that I am not going to be singled out as a scapegoat.

'It's all very fine laying down rules for players, but you must remember the reality of the situation in a lot of cases. I had been out of work for nearly four months in Ireland, so when I got a job in the US I decided to take it for a few weeks.

'Obviously, I wanted to keep hurling, to keep in shape for the Galway team and it seemed sensible to play for some club here. Now I am told there is a rule to prevent that.

'Maybe there is... but I was not aware of it.'

Breheny asked over the phone, before hanging up, when Tony was thinking of coming home?

Tony wasn't at all sure.

He hadn't spoken to Farrell, he explained, or anybody back in the Galway camp. The following day, Monday, June 19, the whole affair was due to be discussed by the Games Administration Committee in Croke Park.

'In all fairness,' Tony concluded, '... I hope they don't take the view that by sacrificing me... by suspending me, it will be a deterrent to others.

'I repeat again... and again...

'I didn't know I was doing anything wrong.

'If I had, I would not have played in New York.'

•••◆•••

THE GAMES ADMINISTRATION committee decided they wanted to hear more. In fact they asked the New York Board to supply its members with all of the history and details of the affair.

The All-Ireland semi-final, in which Galway would meet either Tipperary or Waterford, would soon be on the horizon.

August 6.

The next meeting of the GAC was fixed for July 24, but an announcement boomed out from Croke Park that the three Galway players would remain suspended in the intervening period.

The statement, worryingly, added that the two-match suspension imposed by the New York Board was not correct or in accordance with the Official Guide.

Croke Park officials had their eyes fixed on Rule 41.

This rule stated that players from Ireland intending to play in New York must have their official authorisation, in duplicate, from the club and county secretaries, and the Director General, and that it must be lodged with Croke Park at last two days prior to the match.

Tony and the two lads had failed to live by Rule 41.

Full stop.

And a 12 months suspension still lay in waiting for each of them.

The Games Administration Committee also made it clear that they wished to deal with the affair, before it was drawn out any further. They brought their meeting forward to July 7.

HOWEVER, WITH A 12 month suspension now facing him, public opinion was gathering in Tony's favour. This was articulated by Paddy Downey in the *Times*, who took the GAA's bosses to task in no uncertain manner.

'In the meantime, it is this writer's opinion that the GAC have already driven a coach and four through their own rules; that they are now in a tangle from which it will be extremely difficult to extricate themselves and, more important, that if they accept the New York Board's local ruling without their own, or the Central Council's independent and thorough investigation of the Keady affair, they will have set a precedent which could cause untold problems at all levels of the organisation in future years.

'That opinion is formed on the basis that the decision of the New York Board's executive committee was invalid because it was made on foot of an objection that was not lodged with the board's secretary within seven days of the alleged irregularity on the Laois club's team.

'The Official Guide lays down a maximum of seven days for receipt of all such objections but, though New York are now affiliated to the Central Council and therefore subject to its authority, in this case they applied their own rules.

'They accepted the objection from the Tipperary club on the night of the hearing, which was 10 days after the game in question. Then they suspended the three players for two games (rather than for a period of time), a decision which the GAC have pointed out was incorrect.

'It is also worthy of note that the New York committee penalised Keady and his colleagues not because they lacked the necessary authorisation from the specified officials in Ireland, but because they broke a local rule which states that a player who has been in New York with a touring team from Ireland may not play with a club there for 28 days after the Irish team has returned home.

'It seems remarkable that the GAC can uphold one invalid decision of the New York Board while declaring that another is not correct.'

Sean O'Laoire, the Games Manager at Croke Park, had claimed the day before Downey penned his article, that the GAC had acted correctly. He explained that there was a ruling, which applied to all boards, that where an objection or an appeal was ruled out on a technicality, the board was still bound to look into the matter if it was deemed to be of a serious nature.

O'Laoire reminded that 'no one denies' that Keady and his teammates played with the Laois club and, therefore, they broke Rule 41 and stood suspended, with further trouble still on the brew.

But this explanation did not impress Downey or other commentators very much. The *Times* writer further scolded.

'This writer's argument is not about the guilt or innocence of Keady and his colleagues. It is simply about the GAA, high up or low down, running their affairs in accordance with their written rules and not making them up as they go along. It is about consistency. If the seven day objection rule is applied here – as it is invariably – then why not in New York?

'If the GAA wish to deal fairly with Keady and the other two they must hold an independent inquiry, at GAC level or higher up. But it will not be good enough to make a scapegoat of a famous inter-county player.

'May the inquiry embrace all of the scores of players who, week by week, travel to play in New York without the necessary authorisation.

'Let all the linen be washed at once.'

THE CLOCK WAS ticking down, and Cyril Farrell had sent word to Tony and Gerry McInerney to get themselves home from New York within a week, and join the Galway squad for training for the All-Ireland semi-final.

ON JULY 7, as promised, the GAC met.

Tony, and his teammates, were invited to attend to make personal submissions. They were accompanied by Galway County Bard chairman, Jimmy Halliday and also the county's Central Council delegate, Joe McDonagh.

Paddy Downey remain incensed by the injustice.

'Because of the on-going weekend traffic of Irish players in New York, the GAC

appear to be determined to make an example of the Galway trio,' he wrote. *'The highest profile, Keady in particular.*

'Yet GAA officials at the highest level are well aware that many prominent players – including a very famous Kerry footballer and an Offaly hurler – have played in America without official permission over the past 12 months. It was odd that no action was taken to punish alleged breaches of Rule 41 until now.

'Keady is being pursued for a breach of a technical rule and is threatened with a 12-month suspension. He is not guilty of bad sportsmanship; he has not discredited the game of hurling or the association.

'Players who strike opponents with hurleys and inflict injuries get off with three-month suspensions.'

TONY WAS MADE an example of.

The GAC hit him and hit him hard with a full 12 months. Aidan Staunton and Michael Helebert were also not spared.

The meeting started at 7.40 pm, and lasted for two hours and 40 minutes. Tony had to wait outside the meeting room for the first 90 minutes. Then, he and his teammates were invited inside to speak for themselves. They did so for 45 minutes. The members did not hang around after that before deciding that the 12-month suspension would fall on the three, and would date from May 21, 1989.

Before they made their announcement, Tony had left GAA HQ with his head low and refusing to make any comment to waiting reporters.

PADDY DOWNEY, ON behalf of all hurling supporters, continued to rage.

'This was the first time that any player was suspended under the rule (Rule 41) and now that the savagery of the penalty it imposes has been brought to the public attention every fair-minded person connected with Gaelic Games, and indeed any sport, must be deeply shocked.

'Just think of it – 12 months for failing to fill in a form, thus infringing a minor technical rule, but only three months for smashing an opponent with a hurley and two months for severely injuring an opponent's jaw with a fist.

'The whole system of GAA discipline is a mess and utterly disgusting.'

This was not the type of language GAA folk were used to reading from the pen of the distinguished Downey.

THE GALWAY COUNTY Board decided to set up a special committee to frame the grounds for its appeal.

The next meeting for the Central Council, to hear such an appeal, was scheduled for August 12, six days after the All-Ireland semi-final.

Meanwhile, Keady and McInerney were both back home, and training away with the team.

AGREEMENT WITH DOWNEY was evident throughout the country. Even in Tipperary. Members of the Tipp County Board wanted Tony's suspension lifted. 'I believe that Tony Keady should be cleared to play,' stated the secretary of the North Tipperary Board, Paddy Maher. 'If we are to beat Galway I would prefer to beat them with Keady in the team.' Paddy Leahy, from Clonmel, was in total agreement. 'I think it is sad to see him being suspended for 12 months for this technicality when other players who have been sent off for foul play get off with a couple of weeks or a month.'

THEN MURMURINGS COMMENCED indicating that Galway might indeed take a nuclear action themselves and were considering pulling out of the championship unless justice prevailed.

Cyril Farrell did not distance himself from such a call.

Danny Lynch (GAA PRO): Cyril Farrell does not speak for the Galway County Board whose responsibility it is to field a team. The Management Committee, if requested, will hear an appeal against Keady's suspension on Saturday, July 29th and will do so without prejudice. The committee will not be influenced by any statements made by anyone irrespective of whether they contain veiled threats, thinly disguised or otherwise. The intention of the management is to judge the matter purely on the facts, fairly and equitably.

(July 28, 1989)

Conor Hayes: We have trained very hard for the last two months and we are all determined to bring another All-Ireland title to Galway. Obviously, we will have to consider what our attitude will be if the suspension isn't lifted. I would hate to see players dragged into a situation and caught up in something not of their making.

There will be a training session on Sunday when by then we may know. I have no doubt that we will discuss our attitude if the suspension isn't lifted. I have no doubt that the players at the moment are determined to defend the title. I don't know what the attitude will be if Tony is not reinstated.

If we were to pull out it would be a very hollow victory for Tipperary and I'm sure that they don't want it that way. If the boot was on the other foot, I certainly wouldn't like to gain victory in such a way.

There is chaos over there (United States) and fellows play in Boston or New York or San Francisco from week to week without proper transfers or anything else. The objections are piling up. Laois beat Galway recently and Galway have objected, then there is an objection over a match between Laois and Waterford.

It's mad. Tony played and broke a rule, but the punishment is ridiculous.

(July 28, 1989)

FIVE DAYS BEFORE Galway met Tipperary in the All-Ireland semi-final and started the defence of the Liam MacCarthy Cup, the Central Council of the GAA met and on a vote, that was tightly contested at 20-18, it was determined that Tony Keady's suspension stood.

The proposal that the appeal be declared lost was made, after a two-hour debate, by Jack Boothman from Wicklow. It was seconded by Waterford's Seamus O'Brien. In the other corner sat Joe McDonagh, who proposed that the appeal be upheld. Kerry's Ger McKenna seconded this proposal.

Once again, Tony and his teammates had been allowed their say.

Amazingly, in a tight and tense vote, it was many of Galway's neighbours who ultimately decided Tony's fate. Four Connacht men on the Central Council had voted against him, including the president of the provincial council, George O'Toole from Leitrim. Two Leitrim delegates, one from Sligo and Roscommon's Frank Kenny were against Tony. Mayo's Paddy Muldoon and Roscommon's Johnny Haughey voted for Tony.

Tony had one final appeal, to the Management Committee of the GAA. Terry Connaughton offered to fly to Dublin and attend the meeting, if he could help.

Terry Connaughton: I believe the 12-months suspension is a rather harsh and unfair penalty in the circumstances. It is a sad situation and I think Croke Park should have a rethink. Despite the suspensions of the three Galway hurlers, players are continuing to play illegally over here. Most of them have no papers or sanction to do that, but it doesn't seem to matter. The GAA's tackling of the problem simply hasn't worked and a new approach is needed.

(July 28, 1989)

Cyril Farrell: We will wait until the result of the appeal hearing on Saturday, but I can tell you we intend to be playing in the All-Ireland semi-final. Croke Park has not handled the case well at all. The GAA have double standards. They are prepared to allow the original objection in New York stand but are not prepared to let the two match ban imposed on the players stand. It's simply not good enough.

(July 28, 1989)

THE POWERS-THAT-BE in the GAA ruled, and ruled again, that Tony Keady was out of the game for a full 12 months.

•••◆•••

ON THE MORNING of the All-Ireland semi-final, in an exclusive article in *The Sunday Independent*, Tony declared that he was finished with the game of hurling, in its entirety.

'I will not wear the Galway colours again, and neither will I wear the colours of my club, Killimordaly,' he stated. 'I am retired as of this week.'

He stressed that he was utterly serious.

'I know many people will say I have taken this decision on the spur of the moment, that I will be back in due course. I'm afraid those who think that way do not know me. They totally underestimate the extent of the body-blow this week's decision represents for me.

'These last few weeks I have felt like a man on death row waiting for a reprieve. I had hoped against hope this reprieve might be coming, and that I would have been able to take my place at centre-back on the Galway team today. Now I know I can not even play in a challenge game, between now and next May.

'I will be 26 next Christmas. You don't come back after a year out of the game at the highest level and hope to pick up the threads again, especially at county level, as if nothing has happened.

'The GAA have pulled the trap-door on me, and that's that. My mind is made up and there will be no going back.

'All that's left for me during the coming months is to play rugby... it's the only game I have played competitively outside of hurling.'

Tony was looking at a temporary career, at second centre for Monivea during the lengthy winter that lay ahead of him. He was hoping the club would be happy to have him back in their ranks.

'The worst moment in my life was when I was called back into the meeting of the Games Administration Committee in Croke Park on the Friday, July 7, and told by the chairman Sean Ramsbottom, who had the Official Guide in his hand, that I was suspended for a year under Rule 41.

'I excused myself and walked out.

'I was bewildered, confused.

'In fact, I was totally shattered... if I had an open air ticket in my pocket at that moment I would have gone straight to Dublin airport and headed for the most distant point on the globe, just to get away from what I had learned.'

With no air ticket in his pocket, Tony had gone to a local public house, and found a quiet corner. But people noticed him. They wanted to talk to him, tell him what they thought. Tony left the pub in a hurry, and back in his room on Phibsboro Road he went straight to bed.

For the few days that followed, he remained in two minds about attending the semi-final, but, in his heart, he knew he would still be standing beside all of his teammates when the moment arrived in the team dressing-room.

Brendan Lynskey: I don't think we're meant to win three in-a-row. The GAA hierarchy didn't want us to win three in-a-row… it wasn't Tony Keady that was on trial… it was Galway on trial.

How many more blunders can the GAC make? They suspended me last year for being sent off in a tournament to raise money for the mentally handicapped. How much money is Croke Park giving to the mentally handicapped?

As far as we're concerned it originated with Tipp. They've got Tony suspended. They've picked their own ref (for the semi-final). If Tipperary win this All-Ireland it won't be one they'll cherish either.

(August 6, 1989)

•••◆•••

THE TONY KEADY affair was ended.

And a game of hurling had to be played between two teams who, faster than anyone thought possible, had become the bitterest of rivals.

Tipp would make it through to the All-Ireland final, winning 1-17 to 2-11, and Galway would finish the game with only 13 men – Sylvie Linnane dismissed in the 11th minute of the second-half for a rash charge on Nicky English, and Michael McGrath 10 minutes from the end for a frontal charge on Conor O'Donovan.

It was a game played by two teams with a sour taste in their mouths, and that distaste for one another robbed the occasion of ever becoming another epic contest. Referee John Denton from Waterford also booked 10 players, five from each team. But no amount of scolding by the match official was ever likely to calm the afternoon of Sunday, August 6.

On the sideline, calmness was also a difficult item to bottle. And Cyril Farrell also entered the referee's little black book when he protested

Linnane's dismissal.

Without Linnane, and Keady and Martin Naughton (with a knee injury), Galway still fought like champions and after Tipperary went six points in front midway through the second-half, Farrell watched proudly as his 13 men wrestled back control of the contest.

It was a game that Galway allowed drift out of their reach in the opening 20 minutes, and clearly all of the clamour and distraction of the previous months and weeks hampered the focus of the men in maroon. The Galway defence, especially, was pummelled from the start, with Cormac Bonner, English and Pat Fox in sparkling form and receiving a perfect choice of low and high ball. Hayes and Co in the full-back line were in danger of being over-run. In front of them, only Pete Finnerty appeared to have a solid footing from the very beginning.

Eanna Ryan had Galway off to a blistering start with a goal after only 30 seconds. After five minutes they led 1-1 to 0-1, but there were no more Galway scores for the next 17 minutes.

After 21 minutes, Tipp were 0-9 to 1-1 in front and too much damage had been done to the reigning champions. The absolute confidence that guided them for two full seasons seemed to have turned its back on the team. Instead, there was a frantic, panicked quality to what Galway attempted.

It could have been worse. Bonner had rounded Hayes but his brilliant shot was somehow blocked by John Commins when a goal seemed certain. Less than half a minute before the half-time break, Ryan got in for his second goal that allowed Galway to talk over the break about a dramatic fightback.

One in honour of Tony Keady.

However, if anything, too much had been attempted from the very start of the game in the name of the man who had been unjustly removed from the field.

The writing was back on the wall, when on the restart Fox scored a sublime goal after receiving possession from English. However, six points in arrears, and with their title taken from them it appeared, Galway raised themselves. Another brilliant save from Commins gave everyone some little hope. With three minutes of normal time left, there were only two points between the teams.

English scored his eighth point of the afternoon to stretch the margin back to three, but there was still time for stoppages to be added on.

Except the referee did not add on any time for stoppages.

'From a distance, Galway may be depicted as wretched losers,' wrote Vincent Hogan in *The Irish Independent*. *'... who lost all dignity, with their crown, but they are entitled to a fairer postscript.*

'From start to finish, this voice of reason (the referee) had clearly lost his way,' continued Hogan who, despite criticising the losers for failing to present the proud disposition of champions, still felt like applauding them off the field.

'And yet some heroism climbed above the anger. For even with a full complement in their trenches, it must be said that Tipperary struggled, at times, grotesquely to survive the mayhem. As selector, Donie Nealon put it afterwards, "We're like a team that's just afraid to win."

'As it happened, they survived by a solitary score when they ought to have been in a different spiritual parish. Keating has reason to wonder about their killer instinct. For Galway positively prospered on loose balls in the closing quarter when they ought to have been outnumbered.'

Cyril Farrell: Let's get things clear... fair dues to Tipperary for winning the match. They have been knocking on the door for the past two years. They should go on to win the All-Ireland... I'll take nothing from them.

In cases where a Galway player would be sent off a Tipperary player would be booked, and his decision not to allow even a minute of injury time has no explanation. What did we get up front? Two close-in frees... in the whole match?

(August 7, 1989)

Nicky English: With the Tony Keady affair and everything, they were in the news every day and we came in from the dark. I've no comment to make on the dismissals, but in a curious way they put us under pressure in the latter stages of the match.

(August 7, 1989)

Pete Finnerty: Tipp deserved to win. We fell apart when Sylvie was sent off... and we were just getting into it again when Michael McGrath was sent off. I felt the referee had a very poor game and I was very disappointed to be booked for the first time in my career for an innocuous challenge.

(August 7, 1989)

BEFORE THE MONTH was over, the Games Administration Committee was back in the business of suspending Galway men.

Brendan Lynskey, Michael McGrath (two months each) and Sylvie Linnane (one month) faced the wrath of the committee, but they were also joined by Farrell and his selector, Bernie O'Connor, who also received two months each. Farrell was really in the GAC's sights.

He got his time for comments he made about the referee before the game, and also for spending too much time on the field during the semi-final.

The GAC actually sat until 12.45 am. They were incensed with Lynskey for critical comments he had made about them in an interview with *The Sunday Tribune*, and at one stage it looked as though he might be in even bigger trouble as the committee gave over an hour to discussions on him alone.

Another one of Farrell's selectors, Phelim Murphy was also in the line of fire for most of the long and exhausting night but, in the end, the GAC cautioned him as to his future conduct on the sideline.

AND, ON THE very last day of August, the daily newspapers revealed that the Galway County Board was being fined £2,000 by the GAC, who also wanted the board to identify two of their supporters with regard to incidents immediately after the defeat by Tipperary.

It was alleged that one Galway man assaulted a linesman. And that another was busily throwing 'missiles' at the president of the GAA, John Dowling.

When Liam Mulvihill, the Director General of the association, expressed his views on the summer just passed and Galway's role in it, the Galway

County Board decided to end the year with a statement of its own.

Kieran Muldoon (Galway County Board secretary): Galway County Board are gravely disappointed with certain aspects of the interview given by the Ard Stiurthoir, Liam O'Maolmhichil in last Sunday's *Sunday Press*. The stance of the board and official presentation of the Keady, Helebert, Staunton appeal, in the backdrop of the most difficult circumstances in the county, was both responsible and respectful.

We are appalled at his comments, which alleged that Galway did not seek clemency for our players at the appeal hearing when, in fact, the Galway delegation pleaded earnestly for clemency and understanding. During the debate on the appeal the president stated clearly and categorically that the issue of clemency could not be considered.

The factual position at the Central Council appeal was the Games Administration Committee demanded the imposition of a 12-month penalty under Rule 41. This demand was supported en bloc by the central authority of the association. Given these circumstances the Galway County Board were obliged to make the facts of the case known to the members of Central Council.

The statement by the Ard Stiurthoir that an appeal for clemency may be an option in cases related to Rule 41 pre-empts future decisions in cases pending. It is with reluctance that Galway County Board have responded publicly on this issue when it had assumed the matter was closed.

(October 20, 1989)

FORGOTTEN IN ALL of the furore over Tony Keady's suspension was his chance of picking up a third Allstar award. The rules of the awards stated that a player who served a suspension in the year under review was ineligible for the team. And even though, like all of the others on the banned list at the end of 1989, Tony was not guilty of a breach of sportsmanship on the field of play, he was outlawed from the awards scheme.

But, there was no retirement.

Tony had a long winter to think what he wished to achieve in the second-half of his career as a Galway hurler. He decided he wanted more.

At least one more All-Ireland title.

The day before Galway met Antrim in the league in Ballinasloe, the GAA's Mercy committee ratified a recommendation from the GAC that the 12-month suspension on Tony, and Staunton and Helebert, be lifted.

In choosing his team for the game in Duggan Park, Cyril Farrell had named A.N. Other at centre-back.

Galway would win the game, 3-9 to 1-3 but 10 minutes before it started Keady and Lynskey made their way into the ground and spent the afternoon as two more interested spectators. Tony had been freed to play, but Michael Coleman manned the No.6 shirt in Tony's continued absence, for a little while longer.

••• ◆ •••

TWO DECADES DOWN the road from the spring and summer of 1989, Tony cast his mind back on that year in which he was the most talked about sportsman in Ireland, for no good reason.

He remembered to long days clearly, and he remembered how it all started once the Allstars tour ended and everyone was packing up for home. 'I remember saying to myself... *What am I going home for now? Another year for slogging... for this three in-a-row they were all talking about?*

'I decided I was finishing up.

'That was it. The brother was doing well in Boston, so I decided I was staying. I had a good bit won in the hurling and... I was happy enough.

'Farrell didn't travel on the trip, but I think he had an idea what I was thinking. He had told the lads to make sure that my bags were on the bus. That way, he felt that I'd have to come home.

'I thought Farrell knew me... but he didn't.

'I let off all the luggage home. After about three days I rang Lynskey... asked him would he hop out to the airport where there was a bag still going around on the carousel.'

Of course, Tony never headed up to Boston to team up with his brother. He loved New York too much. He found work with a construction company owned by a man from Loughrea, Martin Bruton. He enjoyed the warmth of May, announcing another steaming summer in the city. Fitting in a few games of hurling, mostly for the pure enjoyment of it, completed the deal in his head that New York City could be his home at some point.

Teams were looking for him to play too, though contacting Ireland's reigning Hurler of the Year was not an easy task.

'I basically had a plug socket... and a phone,' he continued. 'There was a girl in the apartment next door and we had it arranged that the wire of my phone was plugged into the back of hers. So, is anyone called... the phone rang in both apartments.

'If it was for her, I'd leave it down... and vice-versa.'

The phone started ringing... and ringing, for Tony.

'There were phone calls coming left and right. My brother Noel is even supposed to have come down from Boston to tell me not to play. He didn't... he rang me and he just said, "Look... if you want to hurl... hurl."

'Anyway, I went down to the pitch with my gear.

'I'll never forget it... I was standing in a corner, only 30 or 40 yards from the dressing-room. The next thing... one of the doors opened, and out came a blue and gold jersey.

'Sure, t'was like a red rag to a bull.

'I think I had my boots, togs and helmet on before I even got to the dressing-room door. That's what the sight of the Tipp jersey did for me.

'I was out on the pitch when they started calling out the teams. A ball had gone over to the wire and I went over to get it. Just on the stroke of rising the ball... the announcer calls out... BERNARD KEADY.

'And a Tipperary fella near me says, "Tony, when did you change your name?"

'I just looked at him, and replied, "You must have been out last night... you're seeing double!" '

But Tony sensed trouble at that exact moment.

His instinct was correct, and before long Farrell was phoning him and advising him to get home double-quick. 'He told me that it was important that I got home. The hearing was coming up and he felt, if I was seen to make the effort of a personal appearance, I'd probably get off.

'I thought long and hard about it... *Would I come home?*

'*Or not?*

'At the end of the day, I just thought that I owed it to the boys. I had a lot of good friends in that Galway squad.

'We'd lost two and won two All-Irelands. There were few enough teams had won three in-a-row. Farrell's view was I'd definitely get off if I came home. He was ringing me nearly every 10 minutes to make sure.

'So, I decided that I would.'

In the weeks that followed he spoke up for himself, and faced many older men who had risen to the top ranks in the GAA.

'I just felt that the people judging me... they knew nothing about hurling.

'That's what killed me... there was no talking to those five or six people. Frank (Burke) and Joe (McDonagh) spoke brilliantly and absolutely bamboozled them with what they said.

'And I remember these fellas... sitting behind their desks, just staring into space. It was like they were saying... "When are ye going to finish... because we have our verdict made!"

'To me, their minds were already made up.

'They wanted a scapegoat.

'They felt they had to stop this thing of lads playing illegally in New York. They were going to put an end to it... and...

'They caught me!

'I didn't speak at all much... just sat there. I felt that all they wanted was for Joe and Frank to shut up... it's like they were brainwashed.

'Next thing, they just said... "Our verdict is that the suspension stands!" I stood up so fast that I knocked my chair over with the back of my knees. I was so annoyed with all of them.'

He remembered walking out of the room.

He could hear Joe McDonagh trying to catch up with him, and get his attention. Joe went to say something.

'Hold on Tony... we might talk more...'

But Tony knew that talking would get him nowhere. 'I knew by the look of them that we could talk for hours and hours... and it would get us nowhere.'

Outside, Lynskey was waiting for him.

'I remember walking down the stairs in Croke Park and thinking... *Why in God's name did I come home?*

'To be suspended by five or six fellas, that knew nothing about the game... who weren't even from hurling counties? It was absolutely heartbreaking.

'All the photographers thought we were going to come out the front door, but we slipped out the back. Luckily enough, no one said anything to me.

'If they had...

'I kept thinking the thing would be lifted.

'Up to that night, I was centre-back against Tipperary... but, suddenly I realised, I now had to step away and let the lads get on with it.

'Now I was a nobody.

'I was nothing.'

Tony ended up watching the All-Ireland semi-final from the Galway dug-out. In his street clothes, he never felt more of a stranger to all of his teammates who had prepared themselves for a war to which Tony was not invited.

'There was a little grid over a drain at the bottom of the dugout... I had my fingers wrapped around the grid. When Hopper got the line, a Tipp player had come over in front of us and started shouting.

'Hopper was just passing him, and lashed out.

'I was absolutely boiling with anger.

'I walked across the pitch afterwards... fellas shouting at me. I felt like lashing out, and I don't think people would have blamed me if I did.

'But I never lifted a finger to anyone... just held it together.

'Whether t'was going back to my father again... I don't know.'

CHAPTER 6

1990

MICHAEL O'MUIRCHEARTAIGH WAS not to know it, but when he penned a tribute to Tony Keady in the magazine *Country Living*, in the late summer of 1990, he was actually also bidding farewell to one of the greatest centre-backs to appear in the modern game.

Tony's career in maroon would never again hit the heights it had in the 80s. There were different reasons for that. He himself never fully forgave the wrong that had been done against him in 1989. That was one good reason, but there were also a couple more. Cyril Farrell would spend only two more years, 1990 and '91 on the Galway sideline, losing to Cork in the All-Ireland final and then finding himself and his team on the receiving end of a right thumping from Tipperary a year later in a semi-final.

Farrell's departure did not help Tony.

Neither did the arrival of his replacement, Jarlath Cloonan, who had found success with the county's under-21s and wished to mix new blood with what remained of Farrell's double-winning All-Ireland team.

Cloonan also wanted to do things his way, as opposed to the way in which Farrell had often handled lads in the dressing-room.

'He'd break your heart in training,' Farrell recalled. 'He'd leave his frees short... or he'd send them wide in Athenry... and in league games he wasn't great either in making every free count.

'But once the championship came, Keady floated them over.

'You'd have to get to know him... get into his head,' Farrell recommended. 'Otherwise... you wouldn't have him at all.'

Jarlath Cloonan did not have Tony Keady at all.

However, Cyril Farrell was still Galway manager, and the team was seeking a third All-Ireland title in four years, when the venerable RTE commentator, O'Muircheartaigh sat down and wrote up his thoughts on the life and times of Tony Keady.

'It is often said, nowadays, that the games lack characters. We are told that it was different in the old days, that there was no end then to the amount of characters playing hurling and football at national level.

'I often wonder how true this assessment is because I believe that the species is still alive and well for anybody interested in seeking them out.

'For instance, we are within a week of the All-Ireland hurling semi-finals in Croke Park and one of the great characters of the 1980s, Tony Keady of Galway, will be in there once more doing his best for the men from the west.

'There are many sides to the same Tony, the quiet spoken man, the classy centre half-back, the man that celebrates victories and occasions for as long as he sees fit, the man who brought suspension upon himself by playing illegally in New York in 1989, the man voted Hurler of the Year in 1988.

'Yes, certainly, Tony has been in the news over the past 10 years.

'I first saw him as a centre-forward on the Galway minor team of 1981. They were beaten by Kilkenny in the All-Ireland final. It must have been a great Kilkenny side because in addition to Tony, Galway had Pete Finnerty, Michael McGrath, Eanna Ryan and Anthony Cunningham.

'A year later, Cork beat Galway in the All-Ireland under-21 final and Tony Keady's name appears on the sheet of the day for coming on as a sub. 1983 brought better luck when Galway went all the way and won the under-21 title.

'By then, Tony had established himself in the centre-back position and was already being spoken of as a defender of considerable promise.

'The All-Ireland semi-final of 1985 confirmed the opinion. I remember speaking to

Micheal O'Hehir just prior to that game and can recall his prophetic words... "That Galway half-back line of Pete Finnerty, Tony Keady and Tony Kilkenny could have a big bearing on the result of this game."

'How right he was, all three shone and Galway beat the reigning All-Ireland champions, Cork.

'From then on, it was a case of one superlative display after another for the centre-backs. Galway's golden era was in full flow and amid disappointments that helped to mould a great team, consecutive All-Ireland titles were won in 1987 and 1988.

'During most of this wonderful run, Tony lived in Dublin where he trained, hurled, celebrated and shared a house with another great character, the durable centre-forward Brendan Lynskey.

'While there were many sightings of the pair at various hostelries in the city during the off season, they were always available and willing to be present at functions where advice for young players was sought or the presence of a personality to give out medals, or whatever, was needed.

'Naturally, with Galway a high profile team from the mid-80s on, there were no shortage of functions to honour the team or individuals from it. 1988 brought the Texaco Award as Hurler of the Year to Tony.

'There is a story that tells how the famous pair never got to a Bank of Ireland Allstar function a year later because they were 'delayed' in a well known Kerry tavern along the Liffey quays.

'I suppose it could be said that they were anxious to learn all about that particular trade because shortly afterwards they were running one of their own back in the City of the West.

'It is called the Galway Shawl and already the place is as famous as the figure of Padraigh O'Conaire in Eyre Square.

'It is there that you will hear music, get plenty of hurling talk and meet the men themselves, Tony Keady and Brendan Lynskey.

'Brendan's hurling is now confined to club affairs but Tony could be as vital to Galway this year as he was in the famous semi-final of 1985.

'Did you ever hear it said that... "Galway play well... when Keady plays well?" In case it pours rain like it did in 1985 bring an old Galway shawl along to Croke Park on Sunday week.'

••◆•••

THE GAA HAD a guilty conscience about how it had treated Tony Keady, there was no doubt about that, and sooner than expected he would be back on the field in maroon. In fact, there seemed to be something of a hurry to forgive Tony, and forget altogether the sorry New York saga.

By the end of January it was already being written that Tony would be allowed back on the Galway team for a challenge game against Westmeath in Ballinasloe.

A senior official in Croke Park was quoted as terming the game 'not an official fixture.' But there was a caveat.

If any player on either team was sent off and reported in the normal manner by the referee, then he would be liable to the full vexed rigours of GAA law and order. If anything, it smelled like more trouble in the making.

The GAA's Games Manager, Sean O'Laoire, who was also serving officer of the Games Administration Committee, the body that hit Tony with his 12 months suspension, reportedly let it be known that as the game in question was not seen as an 'official' fixture a suspended player was free to hurl away in it – just as he was okay to play in a trial game or a training session with his county.

Just to juice up the intrigue, O'Laoire further explained to reporters that the same 'dispensation' would not apply if the tournament or challenge game had trophies handed to the winning team at the end of it all.

Galway were itching to get their full team back on the road.

It was thought that if Tony turned up, he would be handed a jersey in Duggan Park. Equally, the Galway backroom team were keen to get Conor Hayes and Ollie Kilkenny, who hadn't played since the All-Ireland semi-final defeat by Tipperary, back in action.

Tony, meanwhile, was recovering from an ankle injury that he had received in a rugby game before Christmas. Some newspapers had written that he had broken his ankle.

Truth was, Tony was busily working his way back to full fitness, and taking advantage of a gymnasium in Galway city, where he had the whole of the Galway squad for company.

It was already well known that the GAA was keen to deliver mercy.

The GAA had an actual 'Mercy Committee' that was due to sit before the next meeting of the Central Council on February 24. However, Tony, and also Aidan Staunton and Michael Helebert, had not yet formally applied to the committee for reinstatement. Neither had Kerry's legendary full-forward, Eoin 'Bomber' Liston and also Tipperary defender, Paul Delaney, both of whom had also been delivered the same sentences as Tony at the tail end of 1989 for playing abroad without permission.

Cyril Farrell and his management team decided against taking any risks in Ballinasloe. They already had a stomachful of GAA rules.

And they had learned about more GAA rules.

Rule 136 of the Official Guide questioned whether a player could actually turn up for a challenge game and get his game. The very rule appeared to exclude 'challenge' games for the likes of Tony – whether medals and cups were being handed out afterwards or not.

When asked for clarification, Sean O'Laoghaire said that if a test case came up with the word 'challenge' in it, then the said rule would be open to a 'matter for interpretation.'

Galway decided against taking any chances.

Tony was not invited to turn up in Ballinasloe, and the following Sunday they also decided to get on with business without him when accepting a challenge against Clare in Ennis. However, the Galway County Board decided to apply to Croke Park for a reinstatement of their three players.

They put themselves at the mercy of the Mercy Committee, as did Kerry and Tipperary.

••◆••

ON SATURDAY, FEBRUARY 24, it was expected that the GAA would be benevolent. And such was the case, the Central Council rubber stamping recommendations from the Games Administration Committee and the Reinstatements (Mercy) Committee.

Tony was a free man.

But, just to add to the intrigue – and spectacular injustice – it was also leaked to the media that another 200 footballers and hurlers who had broken the association's laws by playing illegally in the United States and elsewhere, were absolved by the Central Council on the very same evening.

A whole cattle-truck of players were given the GAA's blessing, and unlike Tony Keady did not have their careers ruined for a whole season.

The identities of the 200 players, furthermore, were not even disclosed. They got to get on with their careers without any headlines, and none of them were presented to the Irish public as different forms of miscreants. But they also found fame as players who had served the shortest terms of suspension in the history of the GAA – as they were formally suspended on the night by the GAC, to conform with the association's rules, and then immediately their reinstatement was recommended by the Central Council.

As outlined by Donal Keenan in the *Irish Independent*, *'This extraordinary operation was undertaken after the genuine gesture of goodwill and leniency made by the GAA president, John Dowling, in the wake of the bitter controversy which surrounded the suspensions of Keady, Liston and the other three.*

'But the cynical will see it as the equivalent of knocking men down and then picking them up with concern and dusting off their tattered clothes.'

For Liston and Delaney there was less reason for anger lingering, as their suspensions were only imposed the previous November. Though after the disclosure that Delaney had played in London without the official transfer from his home club, the Tipp defender was omitted from the All-Ireland winning team.

•••◆•••

TWO MONTHS LATER, Tony Keady and his colleagues had another bitter pill to swallow, however, as the rule governing hurlers and footballers travelling to New York to play as guests there was relaxed.

The 12-month suspension, which had hit Tony and his teammates, and also Eoin Liston, was reduced to six months by Central Council.

It was also decided to delete the section of the rule which required players to spend 28 days in New York, before they could actually line out with a club in the city.

••• ◆ •••

THE PROCESS OF rebuilding the Galway team that had won back-to-back All-Irelands was underway, though it was not easy, further compounded by the fact that Pete Finnerty had spent five months recovering from a serious ankle injury received in training.

Finnerty was due back at the beginning of March, for an Oireachtas game against Tipperary. Tony was unable to make the same game, and had his much anticipated comeback deferred as he was unaware that the game had been fixed for the particular weekend and had arranged to attend a function in London, with Eanna Ryan and Anthony Cunningham.

Galway would completely outplay Tipp without the threesome in Cusack Park in Ennis – winning by a commanding 1-19 to 0-8, having led by 1-10 to 0-3 at half-time. However, if this was a sign that Farrell's team was going to find it easy to put its turbulent past behind it quite quickly, Galway supporters would be mistaken.

The team worked its socks off in training through May and June, but by the end of July when they met London in the All-Ireland quarter-final, Galway looked well out of sorts all over the field.

They defeated the exiles by 1-23 to 2-11 in Ballinasloe, but with everyone, including Brendan Lynskey back in harness for another great championship push, Galway were left with lots of worries – especially with how they failed to lay down the law in the first-half. Twice in that period they were behind in the opening 20 minutes, before finally gathering themselves together and leading 0-15 to 2-5 at half-time.

Though even in the second-half the exiles refused to give up the hunt for a surprise win – and they had the encouragement of knowing that 17 years earlier London had come to Ballinasloe and beaten Galway.

In less than a minute, London were on the scoreboard when their midfielder Albert Moylan struck the ball over the bar. It was Tony, in his comeback championship match, who was the first Galway man to answer that score when he struck over within 30 seconds. However, the tempo, and frequency of rapid fire exchanges, had been set and it turned out to be a Galway man who caused most anguish for the home supporters who made up almost the entire attendance of 8,000.

Michael Connolly was involved in an epic battle with Gerry McInerney from the very beginning of the contest, and he was besting the flamboyant McInerney early on. He had his first point from a free in the seventh minute, and then he was involved in the two first-half goals that fairly rocked Galway back onto their heels.

Paul O'Donoghue finished off a goalmouth scramble for London's first goal in the 16th minute after Connolly had centred, and seven minutes later Connolly beat three Galway defenders as he raced for goal, before passing to Johnny Murphy who slotted home. Between the London posts, Michael Finnerty brought off three breathtaking saves before the break, but he could do little two minutes into the second period when Michael McGrath blasted home – an ominous score for the visitors to concede.

'Joe Cooney, Tom Monaghan, Eanna Ryan and Michael McGrath emerged as the match winners,' wrote Paddy Downey in *The Irish Times. 'But the performance of Tony Keady was heartening for Galway, as was the late introduction of Brendan Lynskey returning to the team after injury.'*

However, if revenge over Tipperary was on Galway minds that same month, they were soon left in dust when the reigning champions came a cropper in the Munster final, losing 4-16 to 2-14 to Cork in their own Semple Stadium. Tipp could have no complaints.

Their manager Babs Keating did not offer up any. *'He talked of how "hunger" was the key,'* reported Vincent Hogan in the *Independent, '... how his team had been outfought. No one chose to argue.'*

For Tony, who surely relished the thought of being back out on the field in Croke Park surrounded by blue and gold jerseys, it was a disappointing result. But he also knew full well that he needed to prepare himself for a whole new test. Cork had new blood, and their manager Fr Michael O'Brien had a team that laid down the law to Tipp in Thurles. He had also found himself a powerful new centre-forward by the name of Mark Foley, whom Tony would have to control sooner rather than later.

'Everyone knew it would take a performance of true quality to dethrone Tipperary,' wrote Donal Keenan in the *Independent* the same day. *'Cork were prepared and organised and produced the necessary quality to regain a title they have always coveted.*

'This was hurling as it should be played. It was full of skill, excitement, drama and passion. Only in the last five minutes was there any certainty about the result. In the end, Cork were deserving winners.

'Theirs was mainly a new combination. Players like John Considine, Sean McCarthy, Ciaran McGuckin and Mark Foley were new to this level of hurling, but you would never have known.

'No matter what happens in the future Mark Foley will always treasure the memory of his first Munster final. He contributed 2-7 to Cork's total and earned the plaudits of Tipperary's Bobby Ryan after the game, who commented "Nobody could have marked him today!" '

Tipperary's three years tenure as Munster champions was over: Cork were on the march to Croke Park.

•••◆•••

MICHAEL 'HOPPER' MCGRATH was one Galwayman who felt it was a good thing that Tipperary were not in the team's sights at the tail end of the 1990 season. In an interview with David Walsh in *The Sunday Tribune*, he talked about his sending off the previous summer against Tipp. He spoke of refereeing decisions that appeared to mount up higher and higher against Galway, and he spoke about walking to the line after his sending-off.

'During the game you always thought that this is a match that you were never going to win,' McGrath revealed. 'Decisions kept going against us. There had been a lot of talking leading up to the game and there was too much tension between the players.

'I never disputed it (when receiving his marching orders), never said a word to the referee. That was because I was so stunned.

'I didn't believe I was being sent off.

'As I walked off someone said something to me, something which I could not repeat. The way I felt at that moment, anything could have happened. The whole occasion had got to me.

'Too much feeling exists between the two counties and we can concentrate more easily on hurling when they (Tipp) are not around. Basically, the players from both counties have grown to know one another too well.'

Offaly stood in Galway's way, before they could get a good look at Cork in the All-Ireland final. And Offaly had looked in flying form when getting the better of Kilkenny in Leinster. Any team that took down the Cats deserved respect. However, in the Galway camp there was talk of a whole new era preparing itself to get underway and win more All-Irelands.

Pete Finnerty: It is strange having a Galway team playing in an All-Ireland semi-final without the likes of Sylvie Linnane, Conor Hayes and Brendan Lynskey in the starting fifteen. The selectors have made brave decisions but I honestly believe that the strongest and fittest side has been selected for Sunday's game. It is a new era for Galway hurling.

We all have a point to prove after last year. That was a sickening defeat that we suffered to Tipperary. We let ourselves down and we let the county down. We intend to make amends for that terrible defeat.

(August 3, 1990)

ON AUGUST 5, CORK took their much anticipated step into the All-Ireland final, dispatching Antrim by 1-20 to 1-13, and hardly extending themselves in the process. In the second semi-final on the programme enjoyed by 40,786 supporters, Galway, surprisingly had it just as easy against Offaly. There were six points between the teams in the end, but the overall Galway performance was one of calmness and magnificence.

Tony was through to his fifth All-Ireland final in six years.

He was also looking as good as ever, and in the *Independent* the next morning, Vincent Hogan gave the Galway half-back line close to top marks out of 10. Finnerty was awarded a nine, and Tony and McInerney each received a resounding eight.

'*Galway overwhelmed Paudge Mulhare's crew with an ease that seemed unhealthy,*' wrote Hogan. '*They shot as many wides as scores and, long before the finish, had come to look a mite disinterested. Such cakewalks can be dangerous.*

'*Cyril Farrell will know his jigsaw has his flaws. Five of the eight forwards he used yesterday failed to raise a flag and there were flickers of uncertainty in a full-back line, as yet, not seriously questioned.*

'Cork, in the final, are sure to push Farrell's men far closer to some answers. They will do so because humility rarely intrudes upon their hurling psyche. Cork will not be dictated to like Offaly.

'And yet, the suspicion lurks that MacCarthy is going westward. When great hurling "lines" are spoken of, Galway's half-back triumvirate is entitled to a fair hearing. Yesterday, they reminded us of their beauty.

'Tony Keady's crazy exile has done little to dilute his power and Gerry McInerney brings a boldness to the left wing that few can even imitate. Yet, Finnerty is their leader.

'Finnerty was wonderful yesterday, thundering through the dust like a man ordained to lead his people from depression. It mattered not a whit who Offaly assigned to shadow the Mullagh flier. Big Pete was on his blow.'

Without their inspirational pairing of Brian Whelehan and Joachim Kelly Offaly were always playing uphill. Galway were in control of the game from the very beginning, and although playing against a fresh breeze they set out their stall, only conceding three points to the Leinster champions in the first-half.

The defence was rock solid, Michael Coleman and Pat Malone had an iron grip on the exchanges in the middle of the field, and captain Joe Cooney was simply inspirational. The only flaw, as identified by Hogan, was inaccuracy in front of the posts and Farrell must have wondered about a total of 16 wides, of which nine, all scoreable chances, were fired left or right of the posts in the opening half. At the end of that period, Galway still managed to hold a 1-9 to 0-3 advantage.

Also perhaps, just as irritating for the Galway manager on his drive home, was the memory of an Offaly team, totally outplayed for the longest periods, getting themselves into position to fire a damning total of 17 wides. This included three goal chances, Mark Corrigan twice failing with his final touch, and Johnny Pilkington also misfiring when in an excellent position 25 yards out.

There was never any fear of Galway losing.

Nevertheless, there was more work to be done – lots more work on the training field – before Farrell could be confident of a 70 minutes performance exactly to his liking against Cork in the final.

••◆•••

AS THE ELDER statesman of Gaelic writers in Ireland, Paddy Downey of the *Times* liked to be treated with a touch more than a modicum of respect. He always found that when he travelled west.

He loved having Galway back in the All-Ireland final in double-quick time, and wrote so, without finding fault with venues anywhere else in the country.

'Once upon a time – and if God is good it may happen again in a new millennium – sports journalists knew every blade of grass in Fitzgerald Stadium, Killarney,' wrote Downey. *'That was the time when Kerry trained there year after year for All-Ireland football finals.*

'It is nearly the same thing now at the hurling field known as Kenny Park in Athenry. The hurlers of Galway trained on that lovely field for two All-Ireland finals in the 1970s, six in the 1980s, and the first year of a new decade sees them there again, preparing with undiminished enthusiasm for the effort to retain the Liam MacCarthy Cup in next Sunday's clash with Cork at Croke Park.

'Even in 1980, when they won the title after a lapse of 57 years, training for the All-Ireland final was still a novelty for the Galway hurling team. Now it is a familiar exercise, for most members of the panel have gone through it with only one break (1989) since their great run began in 1985. In other words, Galway are contesting their fifth final in six years, two of which they won, in 1987 and '88.

'But Cyril Farrell, in his sixth successive year as manager and coach, and with Phelim Murphy and Bernie O'Connor as co-selectors during all of that time, ensures that training never bores his players.'

Downey discovered that Farrell, once outdoor training began in earnest for the championship, had increased the number of sessions by 25 compared with 1988 – and that Galway had totalled over 70 nights and mornings out on Kenny Park. Nine weeks of weight training in O'Connor's Gymnasium in the city had preceded this long count. He also heard how, with Tony Keady and Brendan Lynskey back home, and now in the pub business in Galway city, the squad had an attendance rate of one hundred per cent. The only man driving the whole way from Dublin to Athenry for training was the new full-back, Sean Treacy who worked as a prison officer in Mountjoy.

Cyril Farrell: We ask an awful lot of them, and they give everything they've got. Now... if they're not good enough, so be it. But we look after our players in Galway. Anything they want within reason, we give to them.

(August 28, 1990)

IT WAS EXPLAINED to Downey that when the team took a weekend away in Carraroe, they began their first training session on the Saturday morning at eight o'clock, having jogged the two miles to the local GAA field. After breakfast there was another two hours of a workout. After an early dinner there was another hour of hurling. Then there were showers, and videos to examine of themselves and opposition. After supper there were more videos to watch. And, finally, Farrell rounded off an exacting day with a 30 minutes team talk.

Cyril Farrell: They slept soundly then. They were jacked... but it did them the world of good. In the latter games in the league they weren't able to walk, but all of our gym work achieved what we wanted for the summer. It got their legs and stomachs right, and since outdoor training began we have reaped the benefits.

(August 28, 1990)

FARRELL AND HIS trusty lieutenants, as the days counted down to the All-Ireland final, knew that they needed to get things absolutely right.

Galway had never beaten Cork in an All-Ireland final, having met the Rebels and been beaten by them in 1928 and '29, 1953 and 1986. Eight of the same Cork team from that victory in '86 were still in the hunt for another All-Ireland medal in 1990, and nobody in the Galway camp dared to think that Cork were a team in the making, rather than a team that was a finished body of work.

At the same time, everyone in Kenny Park knew that while they themselves had struggled through the league campaign (and would be consigned to Division Two of the NHL for the 1990-91 season due to some leaden performances), Tipperary had also been out of touch for an even longer period of time during the spring and summer.

Galway put their early season troubles down to their exertions in the gym. They put Tipp's problems down to a staleness. The teams had met twice in challenge games. And Galway won twice.

Galway had also played Cork on a couple of occasions behind closed doors in early summer. They met twice in a fortnight, beating Cork in Turloughmore and then doing the same again in Charleville, but Farrell and his players noted a 'remarkable improvement' in Cork's performance in the second game.

Cyril Farrell: Probably because Joachim Kelly and Brian Whelehan were missing Offaly didn't play well. Yet, our backs presented them with silly scores and our forwards failed to take all of their chances. We were on top in most positions but we weren't putting them away. We must improve on that display, for if we leave any opening, any softness at the back and Cork get chances, they'll score.

We are quite confident at the same time.

If we play to our potential and Cork play to theirs... we will win.

(August 28, 1990)

Tomas Mulcahy (Cork captain): It's not much good winning the Munster final if you don't go on then and win the All-Ireland. I believe our performance will be every bit as good as it was against Tipperary. But unless something goes wrong with Galway we'll have to do more than that to beat them. They are a fine team, with a very strong half-back line and midfield, where Michael Coleman played a marvellous game against Offaly.

Galway should now be going for four in-a-row.

They must be favourites but we beat them in '86, and they were strongly fancied then too. I won't make a forecast, except to say it should be a very close game.

(August 31, 1990)

•••◆•••

IN THE BACK OF the bar in 'The Shawl' Tony Keady met with the newspapermen who wanted his views on the 1990 All-Ireland hurling final. He was still animated by what had happened the summer before.

'I know I broke a rule,' Tony announced, '... but why should that rule be there at all? Hurlers and footballers have been travelling to play in New York for decades. There should be no restriction if they don't let down their club or county teams at home.

'Then let the New York Board regulate the number of players from Ireland who play with clubs there in any particular game.'

It was hard for Tony to leave the struggle of 1989 to one side, particularly so since he had trained with the team right up to the Tuesday before the All-Ireland semi-final defeat to Tipperary.

He struggled to rid his mind of the actual Sunday of the game.

'I didn't give a damn about any GAA officials seeing me,' he told the paper men sitting around him. 'I walked out on the field with the team... carrying Brendan Lynskey's hurley, and I sat in the Galway dugout throughout the game.'

But, if he had done more than that... if he had being wearing the No.6 shirt as he walked out onto the field that afternoon, would Galway have clinched an unbelievable three in-a-row?

'That's water under the bridge now.

'And we're into another final!'

Cork?

'I don't think you can judge them properly on their game against Tipperary. A few of Tipp's best men didn't play well.'

Cork's new powerful centre-forward, Mark Foley?

'He is tall, strong... and a good hurler. He caused havoc in the Tipp defence and took his scores well.'

Tony had no reason to believe that Mark Foley would not be his primary concern or that, just like 1986, Tomas Mulcahy would be the man he needed to afford most of his attention.

••• ◆ •••

IT WAS TONY Keady's last All-Ireland final.

1 Minute: Cork's John Fitzgibbon, lying on the ground on the left, possibly waiting for a free, helps Kevin Hennessy gain possession in front of the posts and he hits a speculative ground shot for Cork's opening goal.

2 Minutes: Seconds after the resultant puck out, Joe Cooney points for Galway from the right.

3 Minutes: Teddy McCarthy sends over a long range point for Cork.

5 Minutes: The splendid agility of John Fitzgibbon is in evidence, when, after a solo effort, he sends over a point while slipping on the ground.

8 Minutes: Cooney closes Galway's deficit to a goal with a delightfully struck point.

9 Minutes: Cooney again, this time from a narrow angle on the right, scores a point but breaks his hurley while evading the attention of the Cork defence.

10 Minutes: Tony Keady surges up from defence, through the middle, to score a point from 50 yards.

11 Minutes: Hennessy replies almost immediately for Cork with a point from a free.

13 Minutes: Hennessy again, restoring Cork's one-goal lead with a point from a 30 yards free.

15 Minutes: Noel Lane negotiates the ball over the crossbar from an extremely narrow angle on the right.

16 Minutes: From the puckout, Hennessy is on the mark for Cork with a point from 21 yards.

17 Minutes: Cork's lead becomes 1-1 when Ger Fitzgerald scores a point from 40 yards.

18 Minutes: Martin Naughton begins a sequence of five Galway scores without reply with his point.

19 Minutes: Cooney has a shot at goal blocked then gathers the rebound and kicks the ball to the net for Galway's first goal.

20 Minutes: Cooney makes the lead two points with a strike from 50 yards.

23 Minutes: Lane doubles on a pass from the right to make Galway's lead

ONE HUNDRED AND TEN PERCENT **LEGEND**

three points.

27 Minutes: Galway's dominance is broken by a 70 yards point from Teddy McCarthy.

28 Minutes: Cooney gently taps a 21 yard free over the bar.

30 Minutes: Naughton makes the Galway lead 1-12 to 1-7 with a point from 50 yards.

31 Minutes: From a position on the left, Cooney fades the ball beautifully over the crossbar.

34 Minutes: This sequence is finally broken by Kieran McGuckin with a sideline puck that goes all the way for a point.

Half-time: Galway 1-13, Cork 1-8.

CORK WOULD WIN their 27th All-Ireland hurling title, even though Galway dictated the pace and tone of the game in the first-half.

More so, 100 years after Cork won both the All-Ireland hurling and football titles for the first and only time, they would have the first leg of another historic double in the bag by the end of the day. Two weeks later they would finish the job when their footballers gained revenge over a Meath team that had beaten them in the All-Ireland deciders of 1987 and '88.

The attendance of 63,954 witnessed a pulsating hurling final, spellbound with admiration, and rigid with tension and excitement right up to the final minutes of the afternoon.

Only five months before, the Cork team appeared to have hit rock bottom, and nobody had given them a chance against the reigning champs, Tipperary in the Munster final. In the All-Ireland final they were rank outsiders.

The second-half would go the way of the first.

Galway would hit the front by seven points on three occasions when the teams came back out onto the field and after Cork had closed that gap, finally, and taken a one point lead (3-12 to 1-17) the teams were twice deadlocked.

In the last eight minutes of the game, Cork would gain a 2-2 to 1-2 advantage. Galway, as Galway would do, had questions about the referee. In truth, Galway felt they never had the sympathy or approval of all that many referees.

Maybe it was paranoia?

Maybe it was Galway's hustle and bustle?

How they looked to shake up the old game?

'Why did he (the referee) not apply the advantage rule instead of calling back play and awarding them a free for a foul on Joe Cooney after left full-forward Eanna Ryan had rocketed the ball past goalkeeper Cunningham eight minutes before the interval? That would have given them a lead of eight points instead of five (1-13 to 0-8) when ends were changed?' asked Paddy Downey in The Irish Times.

'Why did he not overrule the umpire's signal for a wide and award a '70' when Martin Naughton's shot for a goal hit Cunningham in the face and spun over the end-line with the scores standing 1-17 to 2-10 (a three point Galway lead) in the 13th minute of the second-half?

'Why immediately afterwards did he not award a free out to Galway when their centre half-back, Tony Keady was fouled and Tony O'Sullivan picked up a breaking ball to score a vital point for Cork? And why did he not note the number of steps taken by John Fitzgibbon before he scored the second of his two goals for Cork in the 63rd minute?

'Those questions, pertinent though they are, must not imply that Cork were lucky to win. Masterly switches, directed from the dugout, played a major part in their victory.

'The first was the move of Sean O'Gorman to full-back late in the first-half when Denis Walsh found it impossible to counter the wiles and stickwork of the Galway full-forward Noel Lane. O'Gorman, playing in his first All-Ireland final at 30 years of age, accomplished his task magnificently.

'He was also brilliant when he played in the left corner. He was Cork's outstanding defender all through and, in this writer's opinion, the Man of the Match.

'The second inspirational alteration was the switch of captain Tomas Mulcahy to centre-forward and Mark Foley to the right wing early in the second-half.'

THE SECOND-HALF was on.

37 Minutes: From a puckout Michael McGrath scores a 50 yard point for Galway.

40 Minutes: Galway's lead becomes seven points when Anthony Cunningham scores a point from a hand pass from Michael Coleman.

41 Minutes: Cork's first score of the half is a 50 yard point from Tomas Mulcahy.

42 Minutes: Coleman is on target for Galway with a 65 yard point to restore their seven point lead.

42 Minutes: Mulcahy is fouled and Hennessy scores a point from the resultant 21 yard free.

43 Minutes: Once again the Galway lead becomes seven points when, after a fine solo effort, Naughton scores.

45 Minutes: Cork begin to close the gap, and from Goalkeeper Ger Cunningham's clearance Mulcahy scores their second goal with a ground shot from the right.

48 Minutes: Keady, on the ground, misdirects a handpass to Tony O'Sullivan who scores a Cork point.

52 Minutes: Mark Foley closes the gap to two points with a point from close to the right touchline.

56 Minutes: Foley gives Cork the lead when he grabs a pass from Hennessy and shoots on turn for a splendid goal in the corner.

57 Minutes: Ryan brings Galway level with a point from the left.

58 Minutes: Teddy McCarthy restores Cork's lead with a point.

58 Minutes: The teams are level again after Lane, with the chance of a goal, points from the right.

62 Minutes: An innocent looking centre from Foley breaks to Fitzgibbon who hits a ground shot inside the far upright for Cork's fourth goal.

63 Minutes: Fitzgibbon again, with a shot to the corner following a pass from Hennessy.

64 Minutes: Galway substitute Brendan Lynskey moves onto a pass from Ryan to score their second goal.

65 Minutes: Mulcahy gives Cork a lead of 5-14 to 2-19 with a point following a pass from Fitzgibbon.

68 Minutes: Lynskey passes to Naughton for a Galway point to leave one goal between the teams.

68 Minutes: From the puckout, O'Sullivan increases Cork's lead to 1-1.

70 Minutes: The last score of the game, a point from a free on the right by Cooney.

A MILE-LONG cavalcade of cars greeted the losing All-Ireland finalists as their bus crossed the river Shannon one more time. Thousands of supporters also lined the route into Galway city.

It had been a classic contest, but Galway had the match won and should have closed it out, however they had fallen to Cork once again. It hurt.

For everyone.

Cyril Farrell, speaking to over 8,000 people in Ballinasloe, said that the thrilling nature of the game did not 'lessen the pain for anyone associated with the team.' There were another 12,000 people in Galway city.

There was no talk of retirements. Not from Farrell or his players, and 36 years-old Noel Lane replied he had 'no notion' of going anywhere when questioned by one reporter. He was reminded that he had played in eight All-Ireland finals in his career in maroon, and had 'only' won three times.

'I am not a greedy person,' Lane replied.

He was also asked about all of the great defenders he had come up against in his time? 'I have played on so many,' he continued, '... that some of them must be dead by now!

'Will you check it out?' he asked the same reporter.

Pete Finnerty: I had to mark five different forwards during the game... their men were moving everywhere.

(September 4, 1990)

Fr Michael O'Brien: I spoke to them quietly (at half-time) and I said only 10 of you are playing. I want the other five of you to play now... and if you don't want to go out for the second-half, tell me. One of the five thanked me at the end of the game.

(September 4, 1990)

Joe Cooney: The ball wasn't coming into me (in the second-half), as it was in the first-half. Ger Cunningham's puckouts for Cork were killing us. They were dropping inside our half-back line and putting terrible pressure on our defence.

(September 4, 1990)

TONY WAS IN the same state of confusion, and disappointment, as his teammates at the end of it all. He had been marking Foley and getting the better of him and, then, suddenly, everything changed on the field. It was like someone had waved a magic wand and none of the contests that were underway mattered anymore. Instead, it was like Cork were granted a second chance at getting stuck into the game.

'I more or less had the measure of Mark and... no disrespect, Mark was a fine hurler,' he remembered many years later, 'but I can still see their six forwards, and they all changed... moved everywhere.

'Wing forward went to the corner... corner came out... and they did it everywhere on the field.

'It just worked for them.

'More days it would not have worked, but... but when I look back on that All-Ireland, I have to say that it just bamboozled me.

'How did we lose it?

'I still don't how that happened!'

CHAPTER 7

1991

TONY WOULD PLAY in Croke Park for the last time in the summer of 1991. He had turned just 27 years of age the previous December.

He was a young man, but he had been through so much, on and off the field. And it did feel like he was close to giving a lifetime to the game. When he looked back on 1991, he accepted that the long road since the early 1980s had taken its toll. 'I was sort of getting fed up with everything,' he considered. 'Fed up with many things going on at that stage and… I more or less went out to grass of my own accord.

'I won a lot.

'I won the county title with my club… won All-Irelands… won Man of the Match in the All-Ireland final. I played with some great men, and played against some great fellas.

'But, at the end of the day, sport is sport… and I enjoyed every bit of it.'

•••◆•••

THE WINTER AND spring of 1990 and '91 saw Galway at work in Division

Two of the National league. As a launch pad for one last big shot at the All-Ireland title, it was not an ideal place to be.

In March and April there was a reprieve from lightweight opposition when the Railway Cup was once more annexed. Though Tony found himself being moved around by Farrell and taking his position at right half-back, with Michael Coleman in the centre. Pete Finnerty was in the No.3 jersey.

Connacht beat Ulster by 1-11 to 1-6 in Athenry and three weeks later Croke Park was the venue for the final against Munster. Only 2,000 people or thereabouts turned out, but Farrell's men managed to take the game by four points (1-13 to 0-12), thanks to a blistering final 10 minutes.

At that stage, Munster had cut back on Connacht's nine points lead and only a single point separated the teams. Finnerty captained the team and in his victorious speech, which was short, he mentioned that he would save his voice for later in the season. Of course, Munster's fightback was reminiscent of Cork's dramatic comeback in the All-Ireland final the previous September, though everyone surrounding Farrell in the dressing-room took some pride in not allowing themselves to be elbowed out of the way a second time.

'*Some of their stars were decidedly short of a gallop,*' wrote Sean Kilfeather in *The Irish Times*, '*... on the evidence of this display but the credit side showed that Pete Finnerty is settling in well to the full-back position and that Michael Coleman is also not very far away from his best.*

'*Others, however, like Tony Keady, Joe Cooney, Anthony Cunningham and Brendan Lynskey have some hard work ahead of them if they are to figure in the big days in August and September.*'

An extraordinary mistake, in truth, from the normally reliable Ger Cunningham had gifted Connacht the perfect beginning after only nine minutes, when he failed to deal with an easy ball floated into his goalmouth from Cunningham. Deceived by either the wind or the sun, or both, he allowed the ball to drop behind him where Michael McGrath managed to squeeze it home at the second attempt. It wasn't pretty, but that didn't matter.

It was Connacht's tenth Railway Cup triumph.

And the team management were rightly looking to rebuild and inject some new blood, with Brendan Dervan settling into the full-back line and, at the other end of the field, Joe Rabbitte adding skill and muscle.

Galway, however, spent too much time meeting teams in the lower division who simply did not give them a suitable test – and, therefore, left Farrell and Co guessing as to the full worth of the new recruits.

Against Kerry, in Killarney for instance, Tony found himself in the No.3 shirt instead of Finnerty, but when Down came calling to Ballinasloe he was back at No.5. Galway defeated Down by 11 points (2-11 to 0-6) and left Offaly meeting Down in a play-off game to see who would join Farrell's men in Division One the following season. It was summer-like weather in Duggan Park and nearly 3,000 people turned up to watch, though nobody left overly impressed.

Rabbitte, and his fellow Athenry man Cathal Moran, who lined out instead of Lynskey, worked hard up front, and Gerry Burke also had some good moments. Rabbitte, especially, looked formidable when he switched from full-forward to centre-forward before half-time with Joe Cooney and he finished with a tally of 1-2, the same as Burke. Moran slotted over four points.

'Tony Keady looked unhappy at right half-back,' wrote Donal Keenan in *The Irish Independent*. *'And he tended to move too often into his old central position. The selectors may have to consider playing him at centre-back sooner rather than later, and move the versatile Coleman to the middle of the field.'*

Before meeting Kilkenny in the league quarter-final there were more towns and unlikely venues for Farrell and his troops to visit and, significantly, the day before April Fool's Day they found themselves in Arklow matching up to the Division Three winners, Wicklow.

It was a game to be quickly forgotten, even thought the visitors won by double scores, 0-14 to 1-4 – and earned a prize of a trip to London for their endeavours.

But what was it all – too long spent in a lower division – really worth to Galway? And were they really prepared for sterner opposition.

In the aftermath of the team's 4-7 to 2-7 win over Kerry, for instance, John McIntyre in the *Connacht Tribune* wrote boldly that Galway would have to rely on older players and even older remedies if they were to produce a winning season in 1991. *'The Galway hurling selectors are no better off now than they were at the beginning of this National league Division Two campaign – and that is worrying.*

'*Apart from drafting in several newcomers, the Galway mentors also chose to experiment with some of the established personnel in an effort to rebuild a team capable of reclaiming the MacCarthy Cup this summer.*

'*But Cyril Farrell and company will be disappointed with what they have discovered over the last few months. Most of the new men simply aren't good enough and most of the experiments simply haven't worked out.*

'*Only Joe Rabbitte and Richard Burke of the newcomers have got what it takes – therefore, Galway will again be relying on the old hands this summer. A troublesome scenario as several of them are not the players they once were.*

'*Tony Keady will not solve the full-back position on the evidence of this unconvincing win over Kerry in Killarney. Joe Cooney is under-utilised on the left wing and Martin Naughton is no corner-forward.*

'*To compound matters, Gerry McInerney has lost some of his dash.*'

Kilkenny, no doubt, on April 14 would help answer questions that Farrell had in his own mind, but in the process the Galway defence would find itself wholly unprepared for a phenomenon who was busily presenting himself to the entire nation.

•••◆•••

TONY WAS BACK at right half-back for the game against the Cats in Semple Stadium, with Finnerty behind him at No.3 still, Coleman to his left in the middle of the defence. Cunningham was still been given time to settle in at midfield alongside Pat Malone. Joe Cooney was out on the right wing of the attack, with Rabbitte still manning the centre-forward position.

Defending champs, Kilkenny looked in trouble for most of the afternoon, but in the last seven minutes everything swung in their favour.

As DJ Carey sizzled.

It looked as though Galway were definitely set for a semi-final clash with Wexford in the Gaelic Grounds in Limerick two weeks later – a game that Farrell knew his men would need in order to further sharpen their senses for the bigger battles in wait. But Kilkenny blitzed, scored 1-4, and Galway's five points advantage was turned over into a nasty two points defeat (2-11 to 2-9).

Brendan Dervan had done his very best to hold the young DJ Carey in check for most of the afternoon but, like many dozens of defenders in time, he would discover that Carey was capable at any time of wrecking havoc, and doing so in the blink of an eye. Carey scored the Kilkenny goal, and also two of their points, in their spectacular finish.

And Carey's full contribution over the course of the game would be 2-5, as he broke more than Dervan's heart.

Galway had led by 0-6 to 0-4 at half-time, two of their points quite amazing efforts from first 90 yards, and then 80 yards, from Cooney, who had moved to midfield to swap places with Cunningham. Cooney was showing the young bucks in the Kilkenny forward line how older stagers operated, and Cooney was also looking close to his very best after a period of months when he appeared to be struggling to find his true form.

Within seven minutes of the restart Galway consolidated their hold on the game with a point from Michael McGrath and a goal from Cunningham, who struck the ball into an empty net when the Kilkenny goalkeeper, running out to clear, lost possession more than 14 yards away from his line. But Carey pointed, and in the 41st minute he ran onto a loose ball and hit a powerful ground shot to the back of the net. Eamonn Burke replied with two neat points for Galway. And when Rabbitte, who had moved to full-forward in a switch with Lynskey, angled a brilliant shot to the net (to put his team back in front by 2-9 to 1-7) it did appear that Galway had taken the very best that Kilkenny had on offer.

But it was Galway's last score, and 13 minutes remained on the clock.

With six minutes left Carey converted a '70', and quickly after that drove in his second goal of the afternoon. A minute later he pointed again, and the teams were level. Galway were on the back foot.

When Michael Naughton lost the ball, Kilkenny went on another attack and Christy Heffernan put them one up. Then substitute Jamie Brennan scored a bonus point. And the whistle sounded.

Galway knew, as they trooped home that Sunday evening, that they had a whole lot of work still in front of them if they were to contend for the All-Ireland title. They had little time to get everything right, that needed to be put right, and at the beginning of July the last thing they needed was for Tony to suffer a bad blow to his shoulder. At first it appeared that he had broken his collarbone.

The race to September was on.

And, down south, All-Ireland holders Cork were knocked out of the championship by Tipperary.

Revenge, and a badly needed victory over Cork, had to be put on hold. Instead, Galway minds had to summon up their tormentors from 1989.

Michael 'Babs' Keating: Lads, remember in 1987, the hysteria was the same in Killarney... let me throw a few names at ye... Finnerty, Coleman, McInerney, Keady, Malone, Naughton, Cooney. Are we going to let them do that to us again?

We are not.

It was a game I thought was gone on us (against Cork) when we were nine points down. I didn't think they'd recover, but the breaks came, and the breaks haven't always come our way. I've been watching Cork-Tipp games since 1952 and this game and the one a fortnight ago lived up to all the ones I've seen. This was a great day for Tipperary hurling.

There has been a lot of criticism of this team for not fighting.

We showed fight today.

(July 22, 1991)

•••◆•••

CORK AND TIPPERARY had drawn once again on Munster's finest stage, when Cork hit the Tipp defence for 4-10 in Pairc Ui Chaoimh on July 7 in front of a paying audience of 46,695 hurling folk. Keating's lads had totted up 2-16 in reply, and 13 days later they invited the reigning champs to their own Semple Stadium when the two teams once again did enormous damage to one another in front of an attendance that was cut off at 55,000.

Cork did even better in front of goal, totalling 4-15 at the second time of asking, but Tipperary finished up on 4-19 with Michael Cleary hitting 1-7, Pat Fox slotting 1-5, and Aidan Ryan and Declan Carr 1-1 each.

It was all bad news for Galway, as clearly Cork and Tipperary had brought the very best out in one another, and the winner was always going to be fuelled up and ready to continue a fierce momentum in the All-Ireland semi-final.

In hindsight, Galway were wholly at a disadvantage.

Untested too.

Carr, the Tipperary captain, made it known that Galway were already on the minds of the newly minted Munster titleholders. 'We'll have no problem coming back to earth,' he assured reporters. 'Galway in Croke Park? We have lessons learned from the last few years. We'll get today and maybe tomorrow out of it... then it's back to business.'

Meanwhile, the Galway team doctor, Michael McGloin was still tending to Tony Keady amongst others, and it did appear that he might be unfit to face the Premier County. His injury had been diagnosed as badly torn shoulder ligaments, received when he had fallen heavily on the ground in a training incident. Furthermore, Finnerty was also in trouble.

He had pulled up suddenly in a training game against the county's under-21s, and had to report for immediate treatment. Finnerty's knee had been causing the team captain difficulties throughout the year. The injury resurfaced just as Tipperary came into view.

A week before the semi-final, Tony was back on the field and getting stuck into everything, but Finnerty, still, was sitting out on any tough exchanges.

Galway, as usual, had received a front row seat and watched as the Leinster and Munster champions were finely tuned in each province. They needed to have a clean bill of health, and they needed everyone on board for a test that, once again, would see the men from the west venturing into the unknown, with no meaningful games at their backs.

Cyril Farrell: They all have one big advantage over us and that is that they have completed a championship campaign. It does not matter what championship is involved, be it Leinster, Munster, or a 'B' championship... it is a campaign fought. We have not got that.

(July 23, 1991)

FARRELL, HOWEVER, REMAINED brave and did not shirk from plotting a whole new future for Galway when he named his team for the semi-final. He called up five men for their championship debuts; Richard Burke in goal, Brendan Dervan at right corner-back, Gerry Keane at right half-back, Brendan Keogh in the middle of the field and, not so surprisingly, Joe Rabbitte at left corner-forward.

Though, some things did not change.

Finnerty and Keady were named at No.3 and No.6, and at the other end of the field Brendan Lynskey was named at No.14.

Though, on the eve of the game, Farrell once more pleaded for a playing field that gave everyone the same number of games, and did not isolate Galway, and then chuck them into an Irish 'Coliseum' on game day.

Cyril Farrell: They can still have their Munster and Leinster championships played apart from the All-Ireland championship. The open draw has to come for the good of the game.

We are not afraid of Tipperary.

It will be a hard and fast match, and well contested the way all of our matches have been in the past.

(July 31, 1991)

GERRY MCINERNEY WAS in contemplative mood as the game came ever closer. He was thinking of the amazing trio – the most incredible threesome, perhaps, ever witnessed in the modern game – and their days together, himself, and Tony and Pete. Did he wonder how many great days they would have together?

'I suppose, when we were playing together, we would feel fairly strong, and confident going out onto the pitch,' he remembered. 'We knew a lot depended upon us. I will feel the same way against Tipperary, though, I suppose.

'The way it is, we are still just lucky to still be on the team. The three of us... we are still there.'

However, McInerney, as the quiet man on the team, appeared to be indicating that the three of them had their days numbered – and that, perhaps too, the days of Galway as a force in the game of hurling was also something that should not be taken for granted.

McInerney, like Farrell, went out of his way to emphasise that while many neutrals might have considered Galway's direct route to an All-Ireland semi-final an unfair advantage to them, it was no such thing.

Far from it.

Gerry McInerney: It is tough on us really. We have nobody to play before that… challenges are useless. We don't know where we stand. We are coming up to Croke Park on Sunday with five new lads who have been playing brilliantly in training. If they do half as well on the day we will be happy. We only have training to go by, though.

(August 3, 1991)

••••◆••••

NOBODY EXPECTED A 10-point demolition.

'When a game which is hyped up as the showpiece of a major GAA programme fails to fulfil expectations disappointment is extreme,' wrote Paddy Downey in *The Irish Times.* '*So it was at Croke Park yesterday as a contest, the second of the two All-Ireland hurling semi-finals between Tipperary and Galway flopped like a burst balloon.*

'*It was not Tipperary's fault. Declan Carr's team lived up to the reputation they earned in the Munster final and won as they pleased. After 14 minutes of play, in which they set up a lead of 1-3 to 0-1, there was never any serious doubt about the outcome of a one-sided game.*

'*At the end of it, Tipperary and their supporters in the 60,976 all-ticket attendance were not too worried about the flop of an anticipated thriller. The prospect of an All-Ireland title now looms on September 1 when they meet Kilkenny in the final for the first time since 1971.*

'*A 10-point defeat flattered Galway – the margin could easily have been half as much again. The pessimism of their supporters over the past couple of weeks was justified. They obviously lacked competitive match practice and looked but a pale ghost of the great team that wore the maroon jerseys in the second-half of the 1980s.*'

Cyril Farrell: Tipperary were the better team today. They played well, they are a team that have reached that stage that will be regarded as their peak. We were at that stage a couple of years ago. For the first 20 minutes of the game we couldn't come to grips with them at all. That is when we lost it. From there on we were having to go in search of goals. Points might have made the final score look better, but to win we needed goals.

We failed to apply any pressure on incoming balls. They were dropping in harmlessly. Their full-backs cleaned up.

Now in this dressing-room is not the time to comment (about resignations). The players have club hurling to contend with next week. We will let things lie for a while.

(August 5, 1991)

Michael 'Babs' Keating: Well, with us, we would only regard today as levelling the score with Galway. We are at two apiece now. We did our homework well, we foxed them. When they ran at us with the ball we didn't dive in. We stood and let them overplay the ball. It was something we worked on for Galway, and it worked. We studied their play… and we beat them.

(August 5, 1991)

REMARKABLY, THE GAME also was not marked by overly heated exchanges, and over the 70 minutes the total number of frees awarded was just 29 – and these were equally shared between the two teams. Though Galway's frantic efforts to get back into the game did incur the wrath of the referee, Dickie Murphy that bit more and he took down the names of five of their players (Sean Treacy, Noel Lane, Tony Keady, Gerry Keane and Brendan Lynskey) while only one Tipperary player, John Leahy was similarly noted.

Tipp were able to coast to the finish line, and do so without their two most dangerous finishers, as both Nicky English and Cormac Bonner had to leave the field before the end.

English suffered a nasty facial injury when he turned into a heavy tackle from Tony early in the first-half, but it was a hamstring injury which eventually forced him to take his leave of the encounter. They was no panic when he did so, as three minutes after the change of ends it was Declan Ryan who scored the game's clinching goal. Running onto a centre from Pat Fox, Ryan saw his first attempt blocked down but he darted after the ball breaking to his left at the Railway end of the ground and gave the goalkeeper no chance with a powerful close range effort.

Though Galway's No.1 Richard Burke could not be blamed for any of the Tipp goals. Michael Cleary, the top scorer on the field with 1-9, had struck the winners' second goal in the 15th minute of the first-half, rifling home from the left corner in some style after receiving a pass from Cormac Bonner. It was Bonner who struck the first Tipp goal.

Michael McGrath, who scored Galway's only goal six minutes before the half-time whistle, was also the team's most effective forward but, in truth, it was hard to pick out Galway men who added to their reputations on the day. Finnerty was swamped for too much of the game to be inspirational and, in front of him, the half-back line was always on the back foot and could never do enough to support many of those around McGrath.

'While never coming near the heights of excellence he attained in the 80s,' summed up Downey, *'... Tony Keady defended solidly at centre half-back for Galway but was caught by Declan Ryan's pace when the centre-forward scored his goal. His wingers, Gerry Keane and Gerry McInerney started with a great flourish, but soon gave into superior forces.'*

THE MONTH OF September was just about put to bed when Galway named their new hurling manager. Thirty-eight year-old Jarlath Cloonan was asked to take the baton from the man who had breathed new life into Galway hurling through the 80s, Farrell, and see what could be accomplished in the 90s.

The Athenry coach had proven himself at under-21 level with the county. Farrell was ready to go for some time.

Cloonan was considered an able successor.

GALWAY HAD TO lick wounds through the autumn, and this process of dealing with an insufferable defeat to Tipperary was not helped when information came out that, once again, cast minds back to the injustice of 1989 – the banning of Tony, and the blatant act by the association that had completely ruined the momentum of one of the greatest players, and one of the most magnificent teams, in the modern history of the old game.

A report in the New York-based *Irish Voice* newspaper claimed that the number of hurlers and footballers jetting into the city for a quick game in 1991 was as high as ever. A report by the newspaper's GAA correspondent, Brian Rohan identified 164 'imported' players playing in 76 games since the opening of the New York season in April of 1991.

It was written that the cost to clubs in the city totalled $150,000 over a six-months period – made up of airfares and 'personal' expenses. The *Irish Voice* reporter estimated that bringing in one player cost each club an average of $1,000, including airfare of $650 and expenses of between $200 and £600.

In the high profile New York senior football final alone, four of the best known footballers from Ireland had played for Leitrim against Donegal.

Two of the four – Dublin players – had played for their own county in a National league game against Galway on the Saturday before the New York final, the report stated, but were unable to get a transatlantic flight from Shannon that same evening. Instead they headed to London, and onto New York, arriving at 10.0 am local time. They were then 'hustled' to Rockland State Park, a three-hour drive from Manhattan, for the final. Both men played the full game, despite the all-night travel and jet lag.

As always, hurlers and footballers were appearing for clubs in New York without any signed papers from either their county secretaries or the Director General of the GAA.

It was less than two years since the GAA had unleashed all of its fury upon Tony and the Galway team.

But, nothing much had changed.

CHAPTER 8

1992 & 1993

DURING HIS DAYS as manager of the Galway team that came so close to winning an All-Ireland title, and relieving the county's supporters of their hard-pressed memories of the 1980s, Anthony Cunningham bumped into his old teammate, Tony Keady more than once.

Cunningham and his team fought Kilkenny the whole way, and some, in 2012 in his first year in charge, only losing the All-Ireland final after a replay, and he once again found Brian Cody's Cats too able in 2015 when they went down by four points in the decider. Those were years of hope, and more hope, and eventually anguish for Galway supporters – and Cunningham saw that on Tony's face from close up on so many occasions as he wished the team to one more commanding All-Ireland title.

Tony was wishing Anthony ultimate success.

And Cunningham now thinks back to when he and Tony were boys, their heads full of dreams, their legs manufactured to run forever in pursuit of those dreams.

Anthony Cunningham was actually at the game when a newly teenage Tony Keady and his little friends got on their bikes!

'I was at the game when they won the bikes', he recalls, '... and the scatter of them at the final whistle... throwing their hurleys away and getting on the bikes they had won. There must have been a senior match on afterwards or something... for me to be there, but I was there... watching him.'

Cunningham and Keady would, eventually, find themselves toiling for success in county jerseys together. At that time, when they had both moved on from their early teenage years and were sizing up manhood, both lads were at work in the forward department, often side by side up front.

'On the minors and under-21s Tony played centre-forward, and he was there to win the ball... be aggressive,' continues Cunningham. 'Even at that stage he had the same physique as he had later as a Galway senior player... he was incredibly strong, very well developed

'He'd play centre-forward... and also full-forward in training.'

Cunningham was two years younger than Tony.

'I would have spent a lot of my time watching Tony... and Eanna Ryan and Finnerty at that stage. They were standing out even then.

'I can't remember playing against him.

'We came onto the under-21s and seniors together at roughly the same time... five or six under-21s, and also five or six minors were brought into the senior squad by Farrell

'He wanted a young squad, and he was very adamant that he was going to invest in Tony as his centre-back... and he did not shirk from telling us all that he believed in Tony.'

Looking back, Cunningham sees a young Tony Keady as a man who would have been tailor-made for the modern game of hurling.

'He was like an Austin Gleeson, he was that flamboyant and natural on the ball, and could virtually do anything.

'The likes of Tony would have loved the modern game, and he would have loved the individual training programmes that players get nowadays. He would have eaten it up, because even back then he was out with Lynskey doing stuff on his own.

'He would have been perfectly suited to the modern game.

'He would have loved it.

'He would have been like Gearoid McInerney, in being such a strong physical presence. No disrespect to anyone else who played centre-back for Galway, but no one I can remember had his skills and his great touch.

'The other important thing is that we were waiting for the All-Ireland semifinal and final in our day, and it was a long wait through the summer. But nowadays... lads have games in May... and they have the Leinster championship, and they are busy with championship games through the summer.

'And Tony would have lapped up that... Tony would have loved championship games Sunday after Sunday.'

Like so many others who went to work with Tony Keady on the hurling fields of this country, Anthony Cunningham saw a man who focused particularly on the biggest days of all.

Keady cherished those occasions.

'In the dressing room he was well able to speak.

'He was a leader, and in the heat of championship training... stretching into June, he would galvanise the half-back line. He had a huge bond with the two lads either side of him, Pete and Gerry... and he had a great understanding with Hayes behind him. If the backs did not have a good night at training you'd hear him the next night, and he would be rising the boys around him to not let a ball past them

'He understood when things got serious, and he knew when everyone needed to sharpen everything up.'

That sense of how vitally important certain weeks and days were in the whole year never left Tony Keady. The tension of a Sunday that would make or break a whole year enlivened him. And continued to flow through him, even when he was well retired, and was enjoying himself working with younger lads, coaching them, encouraging them, and paving the way for others to reach their maximum potential in Croke Park someday.

'He had a very good way with the younger lads,' continues Cunningham. 'In one-on-ones he had a special talent for working with players. If he thought that a lad had any doubts about himself then he would spot it, and he would sit him down and talk him through it

'When I got involved in the under-21s, and then the seniors, Tony was in with us. He came in with the under-21s and, unfortunately, they did not have the success maybe they thought they deserved.

'But he loved Galway, and he loved watching the training.'

Cunningham would see his old teammate at training sessions. 'In May and June, even that early in the summer, he would come in to see the senior training with his children... nearly once every week.'

But Tony would not just pop his head in.

'He'd wait till the very end,' explains Cunningham. 'Managers and the other coaches are usually the last to leave the dressing-rooms most evenings, but Tony would be there still... with his children, and he'd be asking questions and wishing us well

'He loved to talk hurling.

'He was like a kid in the company of his own children, so excited... and so keen to watch it all. But, at the same time, he was an exemplary father.

'He was so passionate about having his children, the boys and also Shannon, watching us training.

'And they'd even tip around with the ball behind the goals themselves.

'As a family man you had to admire him... it was all about his children on those nights. From May on, he would be there nearly all of the time, and a week would not go without me seeing him.

'He wanted to know about the team, what was happening... what we were thinking? And he wanted to educate his own children about the team.

'Those evenings, it was never a question of Tony sharing in the limelight. He wasn't some legendary figure turning up, and making sure that everyone noticed him. That wasn't Tony.

'He'd always be in the background on those nights.'

•••◆•••

TONY KEADY'S LAST two seasons in the Galway dressing-room were upon him before he even knew it. Like so many legends of the game he would find himself having to take a deep breath, and restart his whole career. And, like some legends of the game, he would end his career deposited in the dugout.

Except, Tony's fate was to be sitting in the Galway dugout wearing his shorts, and boots and socks, but with no maroon jersey on his back.

No true legend of the game of hurling had ever been so rudely, and cold-bloodedly, manhandled by his own people.

Cyril Farrell was no longer the exacting, reassuring presence in the room. He was gone. There was a new voice in the room. Jarlath Cloonan had a goodly portion of the remains of the greatest Galway team around him, but he also had young lads from the teams he had worked most closely with, in Athenry and on the county under-21s, in there too.

The All-Ireland under-21 triumph in 1991, when his Galway lads saw off a very promising Offaly team by 11 points, filled the new boss with conviction. That team was backboned by five players from Cloonan's Athenry – and in his first two years as county senior team manager he would see to it that 10 of that under-21 team would find their way onto his panel.

From the beginning Cloonan had to rebuild.

Renew.

It was time for an infusion. New blood, fresh ideas, completely different ways of measuring up a county for a lash at the All-Ireland title. In the Galway dressing-room, past glories had exited the same room with the former team boss.

Tony had to face into a whole new, deeply uncertain future.

Legend or not, he had to win the confidence and trust of the new man in charge – and he would have to do so one game at a time.

Jarlath Cloonan was ambitious. He was very much his own man, and stepping into Farrell's shoes did not appear to unnerve him in the slightest. Sentimentality was not about to course its way through Cloonan's veins.

•••◆•••

THE DAILY NEWSPAPERS had been talking about 'uncertainty' over the future of Tony in the early weeks of 1992. One paper claimed that his appetite for the game had 'disappeared' following the loss to Tipperary in the All-Ireland semi-final the previous August. Another noted an 'unwillingness' on Tony's part 'to put in the effort needed at this level of activity.'

The only man who could defiantly face down any such doubts, and answer all questions about his desire to remain at the very top rung of the game, was Tony himself.

Galway were top of Division 1B of the National league by the middle of February, and by that time too Tony had reemerged and had taken part in two challenge matches for Galway. He had put himself out there for inspection by the new manager. But, as he did so, it was obvious that he would not be slipping back into the centre of the greatest half-back line in the modern history of the game.

That line was broken.

The line, in fact, appeared beyond repair for different reasons. Tony and Pete Finnerty were struggling with injuries. Only Gerry McInerney appeared to have the same legs as he did in the 1980s. Also, the team had different needs. The full-back line, for instance, had to be rebuilt – and if that was going to happen then the half-back line would also be overhauled.

It was said that Tony was in the running to make his first appearance in the league, against Wexford at Pearse Stadium. Though Finnerty was in trouble also, and a knee injury looked to be leaving his whole career in jeopardy.

Galway would remain unbeaten when they met Wexford, a 10-point victory giving everyone watching in the county the distinct impression that the new manager knew exactly what he was doing. And on a crisp, clear afternoon he withheld Tony until the 50th minute, when he introduced him for Gerry Keane and slotted him back into the centre of the defence.

Tony had watched a new Galway team at work.

In the 17th minute of the game Ray Duane crashed a shot against the crossbar, and Eamon Burke was fastest to react and crash the rebound into the net. Brian Feeney was the loose man in the Galway full-back line, and he was catching everything and whacking the ball back down the field. At the other end, Burke and Joe Rabbitte were winning virtually everything that came their way. Rabbitte (twice), Burke and Michael McGrath were on target before half-time to give the home team a 1-7 to 0-4 advantage.

There were four more Galway points in the opening four minutes of the second-half. Five in six minutes. Six in nine minutes, as they made their way to a final winning margin of 2-17 to 1-10. After that restart, Galway had relaxed on the field that little bit as they basked in the applause of a goodly attendance of over 5,000 supporters, and Wexford began to get a foothold for the first time all afternoon.

It was then that Tony was sent in to calm everyone down, and also lift the game back up to its earlier high level for the home team.

Even in the small time he was on the field it was clear that Tony was happy to be back, and wanted to stay and fight for his place. Appetite did not appear to be something he lacked.

However, next time out, he was back on the bench as Michael Coleman remained at No.6 and Sean Treacy was positioned directly behind him. Christy Helebert and Feeney were either side of Treacy. On Coleman's wings were Gerry McGrath and Gerry McInerney. Galway would defeat Clare also by a 10 points margin, by 2-14 to 0-10, though it took two late goals from Burke to ensure such a handsome winning margin. This time, Tony was sent into the action after 53 minutes.

It was not until the middle of March that Jarlath Cloonan and his selectors decided to place their full faith in Tony and start him. They did so for the Railway Cup semi-final against Ulster and, as Tony's luck would have it, the team looked flat and lifeless in Nowlan Park and suffered a surprise defeat in a competition that had so often started Farrell's years on an upward curve.

It was the first defeat for the new Galway management team in eight starts. By the middle of the same month there was a second defeat, a four points reversal (0-12 to 0-8) to Cork in Pairc Ui Chaoimh. Granted, Galway had already qualified for the semi-finals of the league, but two defeats on the trot was damaging to momentum. Again, Tony had been selected to start at No.6.

The teams had changed over at six points apiece, though Cork had the benefit of a strong wind at their backs in the second-half. It was Galway who appeared to be flying on the restart, however, but three excellent scoring chances were wasted – Burke missed a fee from 30 yards, Aidan Donoghue was unable to finish off a fine goal chance, and then Joe Cooney was wide when a point seemed on. Cork got on top. They opened up a 0-9 to 0-6 lead, and from there on actually missed a further 10 chances of scores to bury their opponents.

It was not the perfect preparation for a semi-final meeting with the reigning All-Ireland champs, Tipperary and the first really big test of the Cloonan era.

••• ◆ •••

GALWAY, DESPITE THE two setbacks, appeared to be galloping fairly well. They had topped their section – Division One of the league was divided up into three sections – while Tipperary had finished second in another to Limerick. Tipp were also going to be understrength. Injuries ruled out Nicky English and John Leahy, while Cormac and Colm Bonner were also missing.

Cloonan was bold in his first team selection that had the attention of everyone all over the country. Brendan Dervan (recovered from injury), Pat Malone, Justin Cambell, Damien Curley and Joe Rabbitte (back from suspension) were called in to replace Christy Helebert, Brian Feeney Aidan Donoghue, Ray Duane and Cathal Moore.

With Malone back in, Cloonan was able to move Michael Coleman back to centre-back. And, with that, he moved Tony into the full-back line.

Getting to grips with a new position on the team was a challenge for Tony, but he also had to get his head around something else. Everyone who knew him understood that Tony prided himself on standing in the doorway to the Galway defence. He loved the dash that the No.6 jersey afforded him. Simply put, he loved the No.6 jersey. He saw it as one of the most important jerseys handed out before every game. It was a jersey that mattered that little more than any other jersey in defence, in Tony's eyes. The man in the jersey got the chance to truly dictate the story of the whole game.

Whereas, a man in a jersey numbered 2, 3 or 4 had to stick to his primary job. Plus, a man in one of those jerseys was in a strictly do-or-die contest with an opposing sharpshooter. A man wearing 2, 3 or 4 could have a very quick decision made by others about his future well-being as a Galway hurler.

The stakes were raised – and, at the same time, Tony was deprived of the jersey that he truly believed was his property while he remained in the Galway dressing-room.

Tony wore No.4 against Tipp.

The contest in Cusack Park, in Ennis, would go Tipperary's way, and it would do so far more easily than anyone imagined.

Tipperary 1-15, Galway 1-8.

It was 0-7 apiece at the end of the first-half, and one that Galway had dominated for long spells in front of over 20,000 spectators. But Tipp began to control the middle of the field thereafter, and the Galway defence was blitzed for most of the second period. *In The Irish Times*, Paddy Downey praised that same defence, however, writing, *'Gerry Keane, Sean Treacy and Tony Keady in defence, and Pat Malone at midfield, worked very hard to keep Galway's hopes alive, but without the essential penetration in attack their efforts were mostly in vain.'*

Michael Cleary put Tipperary in front for the first time, when he slotted over a free six minutes into the second-half, and four minutes later he blasted a penalty to the net to give Tipp a decisive 1-8 to 0-7 advantage. Galway, in fact, would only score twice in that whole half – a Burke free in the 40th minute, and a goal from Rabbitte after a great surging run 10 minutes from the end.

It was back to the drawing board for Jarlath Cloonan in many respects. And, next time out, he would have Tony back at No.6.

But, there was one other decision that the Galway manager would make that would completely derail the remainder of Tony Keady's second last season as a Galway hurler

•••◆•••

'A Chara,

You have been suspended from the Galway senior hurling panel until further notice.'

A one-sentence letter was dropped into The Shawl, the pub owned by Tony and Brendan Lynskey. It was from the County Board. What lay behind the notice nobody knew. Tony felt clueless, but he understood that he was being suspended for a reputed breach of discipline.

Had someone seen him with a drink in his hand?

Whom?

When?

Tony knew that his discipline, and his dedication to the cause of the Galway senior team had never wavered, and was no different in 1992 than it had been any year before when Cyril Farrell was calling all of the shots.

The letter from the County Board, on behalf of the management team, did not even include Tony's Christian name. Worse, Tony had not seen the letter, and had set off for training on the same evening.

ONE HUNDRED AND TEN PERCENT **LEGEND**

He knew of no letter.

It had been left on the bar counter, and as it happened Brendan Lynskey had decided to open it. Lynskey, now retired from the team, knew that Tony had already headed off to training.

Lynskey needed to get word to Tony.

And fast.

He looked for 'Spot' Forde, a local fella and told him to get into Athenry and tell Tony about the suspension.

'We were playing a training match,' Tony would recall. 'And I see 'Spot'… he's on the line and I'm asking myself… *what's he doing over there?*

'He was trying to distract me… he wanted to talk to me or something, and I thought again… *I'm training 'Spot'… what are you at?* But it turned out he was desperate to have a word with me and tell me what Lynskey had read.

'Then, a little while later, Justin Cambell breaks a hurl and he runs over to the sideline, and he comes back, and he tells me… and he's smiling as he tells me… "I think you're suspended, you're not supposed to be training."

'I did nothing.

'What could I do? Nobody had said anything to me, and I wasn't going to run over and ask Cloonon or anybody else what was happening?

'At the break in training 'Spot' was able to get to me, and he handed me the letter. I could not believe it. I lost it completely. I walked straight into the showers, and I remember… one of the selectors came in after me, but I told him to get out of my way. I was too angry to say anything to him.

'I had given my whole life to Galway hurling, but nobody was man enough to walk up to me and speak to me. Nobody was prepared to stand in front of me and question me… accuse me of something I was supposed to have done.

'I had done nothing wrong.

'But nobody was brave enough to talk to me and tell me about any allegation. That's what hurt me most of all. It wasn't some ridiculous suspension… it was that nobody was prepared to stand in front of me.'

Tony showered and dressed.

'I walked down to the Shamrock Bar in Athenry and I ordered myself a pint… and I waited for Cambell, because he had come into training with me and I wasn't going to go home without him.

'In all my years playing for club and county, I can tell you now, I never did anything behind any manager's back. I was straight up. Sure I had a reputation for being my own man... myself and Lynskey, but that was just the craic, harmless craic. The two of us always worked harder than anyone.

'I'd never let my county down, and I'd never let my teammates down. I can honestly always say that I never let a manager down either, not anyone underage, and not Farrell and not Cloonan.

'When we were in Dublin, Lynskey and I... we'd often have a couple of pints in The Hut on a Saturday night. Lots of the lads had a pint on a Saturday night... big game the next day or not, just to calm the nerves, and relax. Some of the lads would pop around the corner for a pint when we stayed in the Ashling Hotel before All-Ireland finals.

'Myself and Lynskey... we might go down to the pub at nine and we'd be home by 10.30.

'We'd be in bed, fast asleep by 11.0.

'And I did nothing in that first year with Jarlath Cloonan that I had not done with Cyril Farrell when he was manager.'

The All-Ireland semi-final against Kilkenny was coming down the tracks at a furious pace and the drama over Tony's suspension was the last thing that Galway needed making headlines in all of the daily newspapers. Every reporter wanted to know what had happened?

What had Tony done?

Why was there such confusion?

There were not too many official replies forthcoming, and a dark cloud hung over the Galway camp before the biggest game of the entire season.

For Tony, the shock and disappointment were equally disconcerting, especially as he had worked his way back into the heart of the Galway team in his own estimation. By the end of July he had been named once again at his beloved No.6 in the centre of the Galway defence for the All-Ireland quarter-final against the 'B' champions Carlow at Dr Cullen Park. Michael Coleman had been released from the same position to take over at centre-forward, as Cloonan and his selectors decided against breaking up the midfield partnership of Pat Malone and Brendan Keogh.

Galway had claimed their place in the semi-final against Kilkenny, but they had worked harder for it than they had bargained for – and in the process Tony had found himself in something of an epic battle with Carlow's provincial star Mark Mullins who ended the game with six points. Galway had led 0-5 to 0-2 after 15 minutes, and the game looked in the bag when Anthony Cunningham shot to the net after 20 minutes. A torrential downpour did not help either team, but Carlow seemed to respond better to the conditions and they came right back into the game in the 30th minute when Pat Murphy crashed a great ground shot to the corner of the net.

Galway led 1-6 to 1-5 after 33 minutes, but when Joe Cooney made full use of indecision in the Carlow ranks and slotted home a goal, order on the scoreboard was also restored. Early in the second-half Galway would lead 3-12 to 1-6, and the game would end up 4-19 to 3-9, but it was a handsome win that was hard earned all the same.

Tony had enjoyed calmer afternoons in the centre-back position, but in his own mind he was back!

And he wanted more.

Until a letter landed into the pub he co-owned with Lynskey, and Tony felt abandoned and betrayed by the people in his own dressing-room.

•••◆•••

IN THE COUNTDOWN to the All-Ireland semi-final, confusion reigned.

Nobody outside the Galway camp knew what on earth was going on? Some of those inside the camp felt equally disturbed by the course of events.

Cloonan refused to elaborate to the media the exact reasons for the suspension. An earlier statement from the County Board again reiterated that Tony had been suspended from the panel for disciplinary reasons. 'He was warned about his behaviour the week before the Carlow game,' the statement continued. 'He did not respond to the warning. Therefore, he left us with no option but to suspend him and we have had no response from him.'

The Galway Board was giving the firm impression that Tony was either living in a different county, or a different country, or an entirely different planet. Their statement had only doubled down on the whole sorry, confused state of affairs.

'This (statement) conflicts with Keady's view of events,' it was stated in the *Irish Independent*. *'He insists that he did not receive notification of the warning until a training session on Wednesday night of last week. It seems unlikely, however, that the player will be part of Galway's plans for the semi-final against Kilkenny on Sunday.'*

The days passed slowly.

Tony, after all of the brouhaha, was named amongst the substitutes for the All-Ireland semi-final. He and Cloonan had sat down, after all, and talked everything through in the offices of the County Board, though why they had not had this chinwag to begin with, and curtained off the disarray in the Galway camp, was a mystery.

The media was informed that there was an 'amicable settlement' to the foolish shenanigans. Cloonan's first season that had promised so much early on would soon lie in complete ruin. Kilkenny, rubbing their hands together in glee at Galway's disharmony in the week before the semi-final, would soon see to that.

Galway led by three points at half-time against the Cats, but they knew that the wind into their faces in the second-half would be troublesome. They would also suffer a major blow in the fourth minute of the fresh half when Malone was stretched off after colliding with Gerry McInerney. Tony was brought into the game at that point and asked to fill the centre-back position.

Joe Cooney hit two frees in the third quarter but Kilkenny were level by then, and during the next 10 minutes both teams fought hard and mightily to see who would gain the upper hand. In the end a DJ Carey point broke the deadlock.

Three minutes later Carey was on the ball again. He crossed from the left, Liam Fennelly held off a challenge and Liam McCarthy, getting possession on the right, kicked the ball into the net for the vital goal of the game. The Cats were 2-11 to 1-10 in front.

Kilkenny 2-13, Galway 1-12.

Season over and shut down.

••• ◆ •••

IN MARCH OF 1993, in the final months of his county career, Tony played his first competitive game for Galway since the All-Ireland semi-final and the debacle that preceded it. He was named at centre-back to face Clare in Ballinasloe.

And Tony starred.

Cloonan watched his team just about scrape home, winning the game 1-9 to 1-6, but in *The Irish Press* Tony's comeback was recorded as one of the major positives on the afternoon. *'The return of Tony Keady to the No.6 jersey proved a great success for the home side and in the 11th minute he sent a 75-yard free all the way to the net. It was vintage Keady that led Galway on the road back and four minutes later he sent over a magnificent point from a placed ball and proved himself to be the anchor of the defence.'*

Two weeks later, it was Cork visiting Athenry. And a draw (0-12 to 1-9) allowed Galway to squeeze through to the quarter-finals of the league, but they had Joe Cooney to thank when he kept his head in the dying seconds and landed the equalising point. It should not have needed such a late intervention, as the team had taken a hold of the game, and an even tighter command of the Cork attack as Tony, with Padraig Kelly and Gerry McInerney either side of him, were an absolutely dominant line.

Then, in Ennis on April 11, Galway completely collapsed against Limerick. It was a shelling, in truth. In front of 11,00 spectators Limerick, wind assisted, raced into a 3-5 to 0-1 lead after only 20 minutes.

Jarlath Cloonan: You cannot make defensive errors of the kind we made today and expect to win. We will just have to find competition and rely on our own club championship (before playing a competitive game again).

But it's not the same thing.

(April 12, 1993)

IT WAS 5-6 to 0-6 at half-time.

Finnerty was replaced at half-time as he was unable to get to grips with a rampaging Gary Kirby at full-forward who finished up with 2-3. The game finished 6-9 to 2-12. Not one Galway defender, and that included Tony, had managed to get on top of his man. In addition to Kirby, Shane Fitzgibbon,

Mike Reale, Pat Heffernan and Padraig Tobin also plundered for goals.

•••◆•••

'GALWAY HAVE CAUSED *a major surprise by leaving two of their former Allstar hurlers, Peter Finnerty and Tony Keady out of the line-up for Sunday's All-Ireland semi-final against Tipperary at Croke Park,'* reported *The Irish Press* on the morning of Wednesday, August 4. *'Instead they have chosen Tom Helebert at right half-back and Gerry McInerney at centre-back and have also called in three players who are new to championship hurling.*

'The fact that they feel confident enough to omit two of the top players in the country in recent years – and both defenders at that – indicates manager, Jarlath Cloonan's seriousness in rebuilding the team. Even so, the selection of McInerney at centre-back may seem a bit of a gamble. McInerney is normally regarded as an attacking half-back and it will be interesting to see if he can curb his natural instincts in that respect.'

But Galway were calm and confident. And it helped that in a tournament game in Lorrha, in early June, Cloonan watched his new team have 12 points to spare over Tipperary. Finnerty took the demotion on the chin.

Pete Finnerty: People here in Galway were always sceptical about us, even in the good times. There was always the fear that no matter how good we were we'd hand it away to someone. I'd say they are enthusiastic, but sceptical this year too.

It wasn't entirely unexpected.

I missed the crucial stuff during the championship training and was always trying to catch up with the other lads. I'm disappointed but excited to see the account the lads will give of themselves. At peak they were training 10 out of 14.

I'll be sorry to be sitting on the bench but, let's face it, worse things have happened to better.

(August 7, 1993)

Jarlath Cloonan: I wouldn't read too much into tournament games. But in our situation, that, and the state of the championship, is all that I have to go on. Last week the atmosphere around the county was very downbeat and I was annoyed by some of the criticism handed out to the team by some people who didn't know what had gone on with the side, who'd spent their week at the races.

This week, though, things are up again. There were a thousand people at Athenry for training earlier this week, we've sold our 5,000 tickets and I think the atmosphere around training has picked up. There's a bit of cautious excitement about the place.

I think as far as several players were concerned that game in 1991 was the end of a natural life cycle and we have to face up to that. We started last year's championship without the same two players, one out through injury, the other out through discipline problems, and we start this year's championship without them.

They have both been recovering from injuries, they both were given great consideration and they both are important parts of our championship squad.

My problem is to get Galway over this transition and back to winning All-Ireland finals again. We have only four of the 1988 side playing on Sunday (Gerry McInerney, Michael Coleman, Joe Cooney and Michael McGrath). Tipperary have nine of their (1988) team and that's quite a lot of change to make in five years, Looking back, there should probably have been more changes last summer.

(August 7, 1993)

Pete Finnerty: I don't think I'll like sitting on the bench but I am really looking forward to seeing them play. I think they are going to give a good account of themselves. We are strong where they are weak. I'm excited and on edge these days, hoping to be back looking for a place in the final.

(August 7, 1993)

Jarlath Cloonan: It's a long and painful process breaking up the old team. In years like this we don't really know where we stand until we get out onto Croke Park. Looking back over everything since June, though, I don't see how things could have gone better. Whatever happens, I don't think we'll be discouraged. I think hurling is going to thrive here again.

(August 7, 1993)

FINNERTY AND CLOONAN were both right in their pre-match views of Tipperary, who had taken Kerry out of it (4-21 to 2-9) in the first round in Munster and received no worthwhile opposition from Clare in the Munster final, winning by a foolish 18 points (3-27 to 2-12) that told them nothing much.

But it was close nevertheless in the semi-final, Galway beating their great rivals by just two points (1-16 to 1-14). And, significantly, it was old boys, Joe Cooney (0-5) and Michael McGrath (1-2) causing most of the damage.

Jarlath Cloonan: Delighted. This is all new to me. I'm two years in the job and I thought that we needed some sort of break. We went out and earned that break today. We were shaky at the start and then Hopper's goal steadied us. I told them at half-time it was there for the winning. I told them to go out onto the field and play to win... to play like men. Every one of them did.

(August 9, 1993)

Michael 'Babs' Keating: We were so bad, we were unbelievable. They played hard and more luck to them. They were aggressive and tough. We were so bad... but we came within a goal of winning.

I'd just have to question the overall quality of their play. Fine, they looked good and that... but I'm just telling them we were so bad and we were still within that goal of them. If you analyse our players, there was only one, Mick Ryan who came out of there with his pride.

(August 7, 1993)

THE TIPPERARY TEAM boss, which was typical of the style of Babs, was laying it all out on the table for journalists in his post-mortem of the game. He admitted that there was a lot of mileage on his team, though he still thought that there was a good chance of Tipp getting through and fighting for one more All-Ireland. He was asked by journalists about his own future?

'Me?' replied Babs.

'I'm playing golf in Beaverstown tomorrow... that's all.'

Meanwhile, in the opposite dressing-room, hurling was the last thing on the mind of Tony Keady. It was the toughest, most painful and totally unforgettable day in his whole career. He would never forget it.

And he would talk about it, pretty much, for the rest of his life.

Tony had been mistreated, and deeply insulted, by Cloonan and his management team. They had watched him change for battle with the rest of the squad of hurlers, but they had refused him a jersey.

He walked out onto the field with no maroon front and back.

What Babs Keating would have had to say about the decision-making and actions of his rival manager a few hours earlier would have been very interesting, if he had known what had happened to Tony.

But nobody knew.

Before heading into Croke Park, Cloonan, as Farrell had liked to do, had taken the whole lot of them into the Phoenix Park for a puck around and a bit of a loosening up exercise.

Tony felt Cloonan's hand on his back.

'We're shortlisting you today!' Cloonan told him.

For a split second Tony thought that the manager was telling him on the quiet that he would be captaining the team against Tipperary. Tony was all confused. How could he be named captain, when he was not even on the team?

'I hadn't a clue what he meant by that... never heard anyone use the word 'shortlisting' before in my life.

'It crossed my mind that he was making me captain, but I knew that couldn't be... I didn't know what I was thinking. My mind was racing.'

Tony and the players trooped onto the team coach.

His mind was still spinning.

He went through the motions of preparing for the game.

He togged out.

Booted up.

'Then... I put on a jacket before going out onto the pitch. I had boots, togs, socks... but no jersey.

'Shortlisting you!

'That's how he put it.

'I'll never forget that word.

'I watched the game... still in a daze. We won but... that was enough for me. I just thought to myself... this is bullshit!

'That was my Galway career... gone... over like that.'

•••◆•••

IN THE EXCITING aftermath of the victory over Tipperary, Jarlath Cloonan was asked about Tony Keady and Pete Finnerty, and the future of both men. Flushed with success, he told journalists that the door was open to the pair of them. 'Tony Keady and Pete Finnerty are class hurlers... top class,' he replied. 'If they can hurl their way back onto that team that won out there today, we'll all be happy.'

It was a strange statement to make after his treatment of Tony. For starters, how could a man hurl with no jersey on his back?

In the 1993 All-Ireland final, the fourth decider between Galway and Kilkenny, the Cats would win by five points (2-17 to 1-15). Nine of Galway's scores would come from Farrell's men, Joe Cooney (0-4), Pat Malone (0-3) and Michael McGrath (0-2). Cloonan remarked outside his dressing-room that he was disappointed, but added, 'It was a great experience, and they played with big hearts. I thought the backs played very well... was pleased with their display overall. I thought we had the chances to put Kilkenny away.'

However, his thoughts on the eve of the All-Ireland final were probably more illuminating, and prophetic.

Jarlath Cloonan: A high standard has been set in Galway hurling. I have tried to maintain that standard and if possible improve upon it. In the end, I'll be judged by results and that's the way I want it. I believe I haven't done too badly so far.

(September 3, 1993)

CLOONAN WOULD BE judged, and judged again.

In the first week of October, 1993, he was openly challenged for his position as Galway manager. The team's physical trainer and selector, Gerry Holland was interested in the position of team boss. So too was the Portumna coach, John Goode. Cloonan survived for another season.

At a meeting of the Hurling Board in Athenry he received 28 votes in his favour, as opposed to 13 for Holland and 11 for Goode. It was clear that the people of Galway did not have all the patience in the world, and also lacked some faith in Cyril Farrell's successor.

In 1994, Galway defeated Roscommon in the All-Ireland quarter-final, 2-21 to 2-6. In the semi-final they found Offaly far too hot, losing 2-13 to 1-10.

Nobody was happy. Or forgiving. At a subsequent Board meeting the delegates voted 38-13 against ratifying Cloonan for another year as manager.

And back in Athenry's Dunclarin Arms Hotel at the very end of September, the job of guiding Galway to another All-Ireland title, and doing so as fast as humanly possible, was handed over to Mattie Murphy who defeated John McIntyre on a vote of 29-23.

In 1995, Galway would lose to Clare (3-12 to 1-13) in the All-Ireland semi-final, and in '96 they would bow out at the same stage to Wexford (2-13 to 3-7).

At the end of that year the county turned, once more, to Cyril Farrell.

••• ◆ •••

CYRIL FARRELL WAS taken aback when he saw his old team's greatest of enemies turning up at Tony's funeral. He knew that Babs Keating and some of the lads would pay their respects.

He never expected the entire Tipp team to be present at the passing of Galway's finest warrior. 'The thing that struck me about the Tipperary lads was that they turned out at Tony's funeral... to a man, every one of them. There were so many of them.

'I saw them and I thought... *they must have got themselves a bus or something...* but they hadn't!

'They had all driven up in their own cars.

'They were all there, and they made sure to not just respect Tony, but to respect all of our old battles with them in the 1980s. They were organised and they were serious about giving Tony a proper send off, because they all came in the same team suits... shirts and ties in the same colour on every one of them.

'It was a great tribute.

'And when the two teams appeared together, it was great to see them all... Nicky English and Pat Fox... Donie O'Connell who had so many great tussles with Tony... and all of them in a line.'

Bobby Ryan, Tipperary's stout-hearted half-back, shook Farrell's hand and recalled the mean and sometimes vicious meetings. 'When you think back about it all now,' remarked Ryan, 'What does it really matter... who won all those games... or who won and lost!'

Farrell found himself looking at the Tipperary team at Tony's goodbye, surrounded by thousands and thousands of Galway supporters who, a generation earlier, were convinced that all of those same men in blue and gold were sent into this world to deprive Galway folk of hurling riches.

'I must say, I think the Galway people who were there by the thousands... who turned out to say their goodbye... I think they were also overcome by the turnout from the old Tipperary team, and if it was some other occasion the Galway people might have given them a huge round of applause.

'That is the GAA for you... and Tony's passing showed that there is more to life than a game of hurling.'

A week earlier, Cyril Farrell had found himself in Tony's company. The team boss and his centre-back from the glory days had bumped into one another outside Croke Park, as they both sought to leave the stadium once Galway had outwitted Tipp by a single point in the 2017 All-Ireland semi-final.

'I met Tony outside Jury's Hotel, after the game when we had beaten Tipp, and there was a big crowd around him at that time. He was messing with everyone, and he loved talking to all of the people, and slagging off the Tipp folk after losing.

'And they loved him back.

'He was in his element... entertaining the crowd.

'That was pure Tony Keady. When I saw him... as most people saw him, they could hardly believe how strong and fit he looked. Of course the hair had thinned a little bit, but he was in magnificent shape, and he looked the same young lad that I had brought into the Galway panel back in the mid-80s.'

Farrell knew Tony Keady better than anyone outside of his immediate family. He had watched him for years. He had considered his worth as a hurler, and he had reached an opinion about him as a man.

But, Tony was not easy to determine.

'Tony was always a big kid... there was a child in him, and that was the essence of his amazing personality, and why he got on with so many people. But when he met Margaret and got married he assumed a responsibility, and he did that naturally too and became a great husband and father.

'He loved being a family man.'

Farrell, of course, had not been in New York in 1989 when Tony had decided to throw his bags onto the team coach, but stay behind when the Galway team made their way to JFK Airport.

He heard that Tony was not coming home with the team.

Then all hell broke loose, and then Tony came home. 'There was a while... when we thought we'd have him free to play for us in that championship, and then they suspended him.

'He was a terrible loss alright.

'No doubt about that, because he was such a huge part of the team... and Tony was more than our centre-back. He was central to so much of the team.

'But we had been there.since there mid-80s and we knew that Tipperary were coming stronger every year... that they would also have their day. It turned out they had that day in 1989, when we did not have Tony with us, but I could not say that we would have beaten them if Tony had played in that All-Ireland semi-final.

'Tipp were going to beat us one day... and they were going to be All-Ireland champions. We had been on the road for a few long hard seasons by '89.'

All on his own, despite his amazing ability, Farrell remains unsure if Tony would have made the essential difference between Galway and Tipperary on the occasion of the 1989 All-Ireland semi-final.

'He had great wrists, and he was a great hurler,' emphasises his old team boss. 'More than that, he was an athlete, and he would have loved the modern game... he would have fitted right into it.

'In our day we worked hard, but the lads had more time to themselves and of course they'd get up to other things, and they might have the odd drink.

'Nowadays, with so much training and gym work, the lads are under the thumb of the team management all of the time. But that would have made Tony an ever greater hurler. He would have responded to that discipline in the right way, if he was handled right...

'Tony always had to be handled the right way.

'But I'd definitely say he would have loved all the gym work nowadays. For starters, he would want to stand out, and look stronger than anyone else.

'Tony would have wanted to look the best.'

Farrell believes that Tony Keady would have been one of the greatest hurlers in Ireland if he was a young man playing the game now.

'He came through strongest on the big days, as I have said before... and the bigger the days, the better he would be. He would give anything to be in front of a packed crowd in Croke Park... it was the one place where he wanted to be... and not necessarily down the country, in some old ground, in front of a few thousand people.'

The first time Cyril Farrell decided Tony Keady's worth as a hurler, he was not Galway manager.

But Farrell took note.

'I said that if I ever got in to manage Galway again that I would have him at No.6. He had played in so many other positions underage, and the truth of it is that he could play anywhere... but I saw a centre-back in him.

'That strength, that athleticism, and his amazing skills on the ball.

'When I picked him at centre-back for the first time we were playing a challenge game against Offaly in Birr, and I went over to him and told him where I wanted to play him... and he asked me was I mad?

'He did well that afternoon.

'Afterwards, I had another word with him, and I told him that if he progressed in the position he would be an Allstar centre-back. He heard what I said, and he took up that challenge... and he grew into the position.

'He became the greatest No.6 for a few years.

'He could hurl... and he knew when to travel with the ball, and when to let it off... and on the big days he knew how to turn on a five star show.'

However!

And Farrell presents this as a formidable however!

Tony Keady was his own man, and any other man, whether he had the title of Galway hurling manager or not, would need to properly understand what Tony was made of, and what interested him, motivated him, and what made him into the greatest hurler in the country in 1988.

Tony Keady was not the easiest to work out, according to his old manager.

First of all, Farrell had gotten to know the boy within the man.

'He was a great hurler, but at the same time you could not be sure that he thought of hurling as a matter of life and death. He loved life as well, and I always knew that you could lose him as easily as have him your strongest man on the team.

'You really had to get inside his head... if you wanted to get to know the real Tony Keady and see what he could do on the hurling field.

'I had him when he was young, and he would listen to me. I knew it would be harder for whoever came after me, and Jarlath Cloonan got him when he was an older player and someone who had won everything in the game.

'It was harder for Jarlath.

'Tony's career finished too quickly, and he was too young when it all ended, there is no doubt about that. And it was a tragedy, but I don't see anyone to blame. These things can happen.

'Galway had a great centre-back before Tony in Sean Silke, and Tony had a big job to do to fill those boots... and then after Tony, well, Galway did not get anyone who could fill the same boots until last year (2017) when Gearoid McInerney showed us what he could do on the biggest day of all.

'Jarlath was a good manager, and he was a very successful coach, and a successful businessman, and I've no doubt he wanted to do things his own way.

'But it didn't happen.

'I don't believe anyone was to blame, it's just life.

'In my time, things were different, and as I say the lads were younger, and we had a more flexible approach to players and what they did in their lives. For instance, we could never have imposed a drinking ban in the 80s... it would have been difficult and then you would have had to police it, and act if there were problems.

'It was better to gain the trust of the players and make sure that they imposed a self discipline on themselves. That was the only way it could have worked for me and the team in the 80s.'

Cyril Farrell knew better than anyone that Tony loved life and its myriad of offerings. But he also knew that Tony loved the game.

And Farrell always trusted which love would always win out when it mattered most of all.

EPILOGUE

Margaret

'Strong enough to be Gentle'

How do I speak from my heart when it feels so very broken? Where do I find the words to describe the indescribable LIFE we shared?

There was nothing more wonderful then walking through life with you my best friend, Tony.

I dreamt of a man who was strong enough to be gentle. And self-confident enough to be vulnerable. A man I could lean on who could lean on me too,

And a man who would love me as I loved him, and all the things I always dreamt about came true. Tony was the most handsome and perfect man I have ever seen.

I remember our beautiful wedding day. It was quite simply the most wonderful day of my life.

Tony's dedication to make our home special and right and comfortable for us knew no bounds.

Tony was the 'gold standard' of husbands and Dads; he was amazing, courageous, inspiring, entertaining, patient and loving. He gave me such confidence and strength. He filled me with such pride.

Tony was my best friend. He completed me and was the best thing that has ever happened to me. I cannot believe that he is gone.

I am in shock, and hurting so very much, though I am comforted and consoled by the rich tapestry of memories that we formed over our 26 years together.

Thank you, Tony.

Tony was a husband who loved us all the days of his life and we continue to love him for eternity. He was the best father a girl or a boy could have. He touched lives, inspired the young and was a man of passion, decency and true goodness.

His love will continue to be visible in the lives, character and resilience of Shannon, Anthony, Jake and Harry.

'Heaven has got the best angel ever... Ours'

Anthony

'The Greatest Legend'

This world has some great legends.

My Dad was one of the greatest. He gave the very best in everything he did and he deserved to be called the greatest legend ever. But among all of the heroes and legends this world ever had there is no one admired or loved more than my legend, my Dad.

Dad loved life. He cherished all the moments in life; the big ones and the little ones.

Dad had our best in mind. We were disciplined, but it never felt that he was annoyed. It only felt that he was always filled by love.

Dad was very proud of us, and told us often.

But he pushed us to improve. He acted out of love and a genuine desire for us to succeed.

Dad gave us so much fun and laughs we loved going to matches with him.

Everyone was the same to Dad; he saw the best in everyone, and he was always smiling. He loved and valued life.

I'm so proud to be your son and to have your name, Anthony. I hope your legacy will live on through me, Shannon, and Jake and Harry. What wonderful footsteps you left for us to follow.

I love you so much Dad and I will love you forever. Your voice and laughter made me happy.

You are my legend.

Anthony,

XXXX

Jake

'My Hero, The Legend, My Dad'

I am very proud of my Dad.

My Dad was the best. I am only 11 years-old, and I have had the best fun that any boy could ever have, but now I have to learn how to live without my Dad.

The best Dad ever.

I learned so many things from Dad. The things he taught me will help me grow, and the things he has taught me show me that yellow and blue makes green. I know how to say thank you and ask by saying please. He gave me kisses and held me tight. When I got hurt he kissed me better and made the pain go away.

I wish he could kiss me now and make this big pain go away.

Dad, me and you were like donkey and Shrek; we were always together, laughing, having fun, and I never thought it would ever end. There was so much more we had to do. We were only beginning.

I wear the number six jersey, just like you, and I want you to be proud of me.

You always made me feel I was the best.

But you were the best Dad, you were 'Da Man.'

I am so lonely without you.

 I love and miss you so much.

 My Dad, my Hero.

Jake,

XXXX

Harry

Dear Daddy,

This is the first time I have ever written about you, or to you. If you only knew how those little moments with you mattered to me.

I love you so much, too much.

It's supposed to be in the title of this note, but I sit here and it just won't come out. I miss you so much. I want my Daddy back.

I want that big, strong, happy man to come back through that door and wrap me up again, and make me laugh. Daddy, you played like a kid with me. You were my best friend, and you protected me like a bodyguard.

I still wake up in the morning thinking this is a nightmare, and that you're not really gone. At night, I look at the sky and make a wish on the brightest star I see and I believe it is you.

Dad, you taught me how to walk. You taught me how to talk. You taught me how to throw a ball. You taught me how to hurl.

But you didn't teach me how to live without you.

I miss you very, very much, and I love you to the moon and back. And what I would give to sit on your knee just one more time, or to have one of those great big hugs of yours.

All my love, Daddy.
Harry,
XXXX

Shannon

It's hard to know where to begin.

What happened on August 9… I thought was never going to happen.

I never expected, at my age, to pick a coffin for my Daddy to rest in. Every morning waking up and every night going to bed, my heart breaks and hurts that bit more.

I still wake up and forget what has happened.

I think you're just going to call me, walk into the house or I'll just hear you talking. I never wanted to know what it would feel like to be missing you.

Words will never describe how much Dad meant to us, and to everyone. Dad was bigger than life, he was so fit and strong. He was everyone's idol and the greatest centre-back of all time. He was a warrior and a legend on the pitch, but a bigger legend off it.

You made everyone laugh. You lit up any place you were in, and everyone loved your company, but we treasured it the most. You were the most kind and caring man I've ever met, and you'd do anything for anyone you knew.

You always looked handsome, and as ever with a massive smile and an amazing personality. Anywhere we went with you Dad, you were so well known, and we were always so proud to be in your company.

My Daddy is my best friend, and we did so much together.

The bond we shared together; it was so strong, like no other.

We could read each other like a book.

We thought the same way, and liked and disliked the same things. I will never be able to thank you enough Daddy for all you've done for Mammy, the boys and I.

You're the biggest role model in our lives. The unending love you have left behind will always linger on within us.

When I'd cry, you would be there to wipe my tears.

When I'd laugh, you would be there to laugh with me.

When I felt down and something wasn't right, you would be the first to come to me because no matter you were always there for me, by my side.

The pain I feel at not being able to hear your voice, hear your laugh, see your smile, hold your hand or talk to you, is bringing me down. But the memories we had together, everything you taught me, and the songs you sang to me and the stories you told me, they're keeping me going.

Every day I try my best to make you the proudest Dad in the world, whether I'm at home, in school or on the pitch.

The hole in my heart when I look to the sideline and do not see you standing there hurts, but I know you're with me every day and will continue to be my biggest fan, because you always believed in me.

There are days in this world, Dad that are unbearable without you and can drag me right down, because the gentleness of your voice and comfort of your hugs are no longer there to cheer me up. And the chill I get walking the corridors in school are so tough knowing you aren't around, somewhere.

Having both you and Mammy working in my school was a dream. I'd always hear you coming along, singing away to yourself, and if there is a song to be sang as you would say… 'There was no better man than yourself.'

Because you didn't care what other people thought about you. There'd always be a line of students following you in school and I know you only loved the craic, and that's what they loved too.

The foundation stones that you set down for me and the boys are so solid. You have taught Anthony, Jake, Harry and myself all we know. It's upsetting to look at our three little mini 'Tonys'.

They're so young.

To see their little faces, and to think they've to grow up without their Daddy, and to look at Mammy and know half her heart is missing without her husband is so hard.

But you showed us how to be strong, brave, wise, respectful, honest, kind, independent, loving and massive hurlers… all the things that you were.

You showed us how to respect each other, but most importantly the love you have for Mammy was endless. When I woke up every morning to see you two lovebirds sitting at the bottom of the table, with a cup of tea and coffee, laughing away, showed me that the key to life is family and love.

There wasn't a thing you wouldn't do for us, and everyone knew how important your family was to you. Daddy, you are the rock in our family that holds us all up and you were someone we could lean on when the going got tough.

I know that there will be days ahead when I will deeply miss you... the twins Confirmation, or when you would have been there to walk me up the aisle, or when the three boys will wear the Galway jersey. All the matches ahead of me in the maroon jersey, and all the All-Irelands ahead of all of us, just like you had.

As the days go on life is getting tougher without my best friend. I'm realising there's little things I just can't do without you.

I did not know what it meant to miss someone, not until I reached out for your hand many times and it wasn't there.

I promise to take on your most important responsibility of looking after Mammy, the boys and our home, and I will... just the way I know you would do it.

I watched and learned from you every day and I can carry on doing what you did because no one will know better than me. You will always be the biggest influence in my life on and off the pitch, you're my role model, my mentor, my best friend, my Daddy and, most of all, my hero.

You knew what to do to make my wishes come true, by just being you. There isn't a day I won't think about you, and a tear won't fall.

There was one thing I was never taught and will never learn, and that's how to live without you.

You were no ordinary Dad.

You were the best, and you're my Dad. As your only daughter I am so proud to tell the world that you're my father. I'm not saying goodbye to you Daddy because you're always going to be with me.

I love you Daddy with all my heart and always will. If only my love and tears could bring you back, you'd be here now. Your understanding heart, courage, strength, and heroic love.

I'll always be Daddy's little girl no matter what.

I just don't think God realises he took my best friend away from me. Until we meet again and have another one of our hugs, and you do your curl in my hair.

Love always,
Shannon,
XXXX